Perspectives on Liberal Education

About the Authors

Edwin Harwood
  Professor of Sociology and Department Chairman*
Willis Glover
  Professor of History
Dan Quisenberry
  Associate Professor of Physics and Department Chairman
Theodore Nordenhaug
  Roberts Professor of Philosophy and Department Chairman
Joseph Claxton
  Professor of Law and Assistant Dean of Walter F. George School
  of Law
Marjorie Davis
  Associate Professor of English and Director of the Writing Program
Charles Schroeder
  Vice President for Student Affairs, St. Louis University
  (previously Dean of Students, Mercer)
Kurt Corriher
  Assistant Professor of German
Adrienne Bond
  Assistant Professor of English

The Editors

JoAnna Watson, Assistant Dean of College of Liberal Arts for
  Community Education and Summer School
Rex Stevens, Assistant to the President and Assistant Professor
  of Philosophy

*College of Liberal Arts, of Mercer University, except as noted.

**Perspectives on
Liberal Education**

Pioneers and Pallbearers

edited by
JoAnna M. Watson
and
Rex P. Stevens

Mercer
University
Press

Copyright © 1982
Mercer University Press
Macon, GA 31207
All rights reserved
Printed in the United States of America

All books published by Mercer University Press are produced
on acid-free paper which exceeds the minimum standards set by
the National Historical Publications and Records Commission.

Library of Congress Cataloging in Publication Data

Main entry under title:

Perspectives on liberal education.

    Consists of essays written by faculty members of Mercer University.
Includes index.
    Contents: Introduction / by JoAnna Watson and Rex Stevens—Liberal
education and the Christian intellectual tradition / by Willis B. Glover—
Science as a liberal arts discipline / by Dan R. Quisenberry—[etc.]
    1. Education, Humanistic—Addresses, essays, lectures. I. Watson,
JoAnna M.   II. Stevens, Rex Patrick, 1942-   III. Mercer University.

LC1011.P48   1982   370.11′2   82-8115
ISBN 0-86554-056-X   AACR2

Contents

Preface

The essays in this volume were written by members of the faculty of Mercer University. The essays originally were written to be presented in a Master of Liberal Studies program. The editors were jointly responsible for preparing the materials for a course entitled "The History and Philosophy of the Liberal Arts." We invited faculty members to offer their own conceptions of liberal arts to the students in that class. Essays were written, presented to the class, and criticized by the students and other faculty members. The essays were revised following discussions of them. The quality of the resulting work was evident to everyone.

We asked the dean of the college, Dr. Rollin Armour, to subsidize the publication of the essays. Dean Armour was interested in making the work available to the entire faculty of the college for review before final publication. A loose-leaf edition of the manuscript was distributed to faculty and staff. Further criticisms necessitated later revisions in the manuscript. Finally we distributed the manuscript to outside readers, and made the arrangements for publication with Mercer University Press. This volume is the result of that process.

It is appropriate to record our sincere thanks to all who made this volume possible: the authors of the essays themselves; students, faculty, and others who criticized the essays and made valuable suggestions; and to Dean Armour for his encouragement and support.

JoAnna Watson
and Rex Stevens
Mercer University, 1982

Introduction

JoAnna Watson
and Rex Stevens

Liberal arts education suffers today not because it has been neglected in the literature, or because it has been over-talked. It suffers because the *idea of liberty* on which it rests has been gradually subordinated to the political, economic, and religious conditions in which efforts are made to realize it.

The visions of liberty, so compelling in their innocence, prove to be fragile under the pressures of practice; and as the visions dim, the constraints that darken them capture and then imprison our imaginations within the confines of habits and rules. We begin by conceiving of freedom as boundless spontaneity. We soon say that freedom is license without law. The ideal is pared down. After numerous qualifications freedom is conceived as what is left after all the practical constraints on thought and action have been identified and defined. The process by which this erosion takes place arrests our attention. Finally those who wish to write or speak of freedom innocently, are reminded of their obligations to consider the practical realities which are believed to be more important. The same thing happens to the ideals of liberal arts education.

Though it sounds trite to say it, the liberal arts educate us to be free. Yet freedom in education is generally considered to be a risky, if not dangerous, idea. The problem with it, so many urge, is that such freedom disrupts the normal routines of teaching and learning. When business cannot be usual, people long for the comforts of settled practice. The more comfortable a place is, the more difficult it is to realize the ideals of freedom, because comfortable habits are deeply ingrained. This paradox is noticeable in liberal arts colleges.

In places where the concern for liberal arts is the most stridently expressed, students, faculty, and administrators are often least willing to experiment with educational methods in or out of the classroom. Instead, they defend their settled postures by carefully articulating their personal and pedagogical habits of thought and action. When asked for their educational *ideals*, they offer up descriptions of their daily routines, expecting others to be inspired by their habits.

Habits of various kinds constitute the stock-in-trade of most institutions of higher learning. Often, therefore, discussions of liberal arts education begin with a succession of apologies intended to win the favor of those naturally suspicious of liberty in any of its purest incarnations. The liberal arts, it is often argued, should form the center of our curricula, or *at least a portion of that center*. The defensiveness of this argument is all too apparent. The ideals of liberal arts education should need no elaborate defense. One should apologize instead for weakness in the face of practical difficulties, or for the dissipations of resolve. Our failures to realize the ideals of liberal arts education however, are due less to unfavorable practical conditions than to our reluctance to think about those ideals innocently. The present volume of essays is offered as one attempt to overcome that reluctance. Discussion should begin with beginnings, with the basics. Willis Glover's essay—"Liberal Education and the Christian Intellectual Tradition"—does just that.

Glover addresses a root problem: What does liberal education mean? It is one thing to argue that liberal education is under siege in the latter part of the twentieth century; it is an altogether more desperate tack to argue that we no longer even know what it is that appears to be under siege. A liberal education should be an initiation ceremony, the author asserts, not a preparation for participation in Western Civilization, but the why of that participation. Unfortunately, Glover claims, the threads of our cultural heritage are broken. Herein lies the problem for liberal learning in today's world: we have lost interest in liberal education for it has lost its relevance for us.

"Liberal education at its best transcends the merely intellectual," Glover says; "it needs to involve the student in some kind of personal commitment to values basic in his cultural tradition. In short, there is an inescapable *religious* dimension in the best liberal education just as there is an inescapable religious dimension in any live culture." Glover's thesis is that we have failed to appreciate the extent of the influence of the Christian tradition on the development of Western Civilization. In fact, the beginnings of Enlightenment are marked by the repudiation of Christianity by the intellectual leadership, so that "the situation we now face is a fundamental dichotomy between Christianity and various forms of atheistic humanism."

Glover sees the disagreements as less significant for the development of liberal education than what these faiths have in common. When we can understand that both the Christian and humanistic structures of the Western mind are founded in the biblical-Christian tradition, then a frank approach to intellectual history is possible. The revitalization of liberal education will occur when we reembrace our roots in the biblical-Christian tradition. Not only will a critical backdrop for the initiate be drawn, but the tradition will instill in us our historical responsibilities for the future. There, points the author, is the source for the relevance of liberal education for us today.

A scientist once quipped, "Because we have a class of specific subjects which we call the humanities, I have often felt, therefore, that my discipline must fall into a class of subjects known as the inhumanities." Away with battlelines!, calls Dan Quisenberry in his essay, "Science as a Liberal Arts Discipline." The case is simply put: science provides a framework on which we construct our civilization. "That an understanding of science is vital, in a liberal arts environment," says the author, "comes with the realization that the physical world is domain for all human experience, and nature places virtually absolute conditions on how we may operate within this domain." Science gives us means to know our physical universe for it is a method for describing, creating, and understanding human experience.

A place for science in a liberal arts curriculum does not conflict at all with Glover's treatment of the subject. According to Glover, the epistemological breakthrough that opened the way to modern science is rooted in the biblical tradition. Further, the futuristic orientation places squarely upon the shoulders of science a requirement to provide means to order and regularize our world. The fact that we can hope to know what may happen next has not only made science possible, but can make a future possible. It is not an issue of determinism or causality, much less control, but an issue of preparedness. Glover's essay speaks to one aspect of preparedness, and Quisenberry's, to another. Both speak to the importance of liberal education.

It is not enough that we may have a rubric and a methodology. Liberal education is a business of people teaching and people learning in an institutionalized setting. At this point, a much discussed question arises: are persons engaged in teaching and learning the victims of institutions, or are institutions of higher learning the victims of such persons? Kurt Corriher is persuaded of the latter: "Of course, it is people who fail, not institutions." In his "American Leadership and the Failure of the Humanities," Corriher argues that our society has suffered irrevocably for lack of creative leadership which it is the task of institutions of higher learning to provide. Liberal education should "produce not mere competence, but stature as well." According to the author, the cadre of technician-managers who form the American leadership caste lacks a historical and cultural perspective, due not to the failure of liberal education to provide the perspective, but often the failure of future leaders' college curriculum to embrace it.

But the problem goes beyond that, Corriher argues. The very people—the liberal arts scholars and teachers—who bemoan the state of learning today are responsible for that condition. College faculty have a stereotyped image which generates little respect in the "real world" of practical affairs. This unflattering stereotype of a "harmless, absentminded professor"—combined with a history in this country of entrenched anti-intellectualism—is allowed by college faculty to persist. The scorn of faculty for life outside the walls of academe is reciprocated. For example, the business community has as little respect for a community of liberal learning as the liberal educators have for the world of business. Liberal arts institutions must evoke a new image, says Corriher, in which the faculty must necessarily play a crucial role. The humanities especially need a new vigor. The good of society and the good of institutions of liberal education are inextricably tied. The author challenges liberal arts faculty to seek their raison d'etre.

Purpose is the cornerstone of the essay by Theodore Nordenhaug,

"Where Have All the Flowers Gone?," an essay about institutions. Institutions of higher learning, the author contends, have lost their purpose. But the twentieth century is a time when many things ended, although they did not stop. In this world—including the world of higher education—much merely survives. Can the academy keep going without purpose, without belief? Yes, Nordenhaug says, because the survival powers of institutions are amazing!

At what point is the taking on of new functions by an institution no longer adaptation but something wholly different? If the definition of liberal learning is "education that liberates," then how far can college faculty go, Nordenhaug asks, before the notion of liberation has been stretched too far? The author challenges the argument that the learning of skills is liberating. At best, skills-acquisition is a survival technique. "Say the skills-people, it is the main job of liberal learning to teach skills, because if people acquire the right skills then they can get all the facts they want whenever they want them." Institutions of liberal education can no longer teach facts because there are too many. Therefore, skills-development is an adaptation by educators in order to survive the Great Knowledge Explosion—a development that marks the beginning of the end of higher learning, according to the author.

The amount of factual information to which modern man has access is a part of Adrienne Bond's concern in her essay, "The Arts that Liberate: Labeling the Black Box." For Bond, the way to deal with the information explosion is more by developing sophisticated means for mediating information and less by developing skills for the management of information. Liberal education, Bond suggests, is learning which liberates students from manipulation by information merchants by improving students' ability to understand and use language.

One dimension in this learning process is somehow to come to grips with different modes of thinking. In an age of the language of facts, for example, novelists walk a thin line between the "tongues of men" and the "tongues of angels." Liberal arts faculty also walk a line between the teaching of technique whereby the spirit of liberal education may be lost, and the teaching of concepts whereby the student may be lost. Ideally, liberal education would provide a variety of approaches to truth because "truth can only be approached, not ascertained," suggests the author. A liberal arts institution should be an "interpretive community." This is what liberal education must be about, insists Bond.

A task or purpose for liberal education is necessary. Yet, agreement on that purpose (which would be remarkable in itself) takes us only part of the way. Bond uses the "black box" to close her discussion on the purpose of liberal learning. The essay by Marjorie Davis and Charles Schroeder offers an interesting look at some of the nuts and bolts in the black box. Their essay title, "New Students: Threat or Challenge?" introduces a perspective that is not addressed elsewhere in these essays—the typical liberal arts student in college today.

Davis and Schroeder pose a dilemma: how do colleges promote the traditional values of liberal education to a nontraditional body of students. Today's students are nontraditional in two respects, according to Davis and Schroeder. First, many come to college primarily to obtain a better job. The job forecast is no longer sunny. This undoubtedly affects the student's focus while in college. Second, students today are different in respect to learning styles. Traditional students were imaginative, could grasp abstractions and possessed independence of thought. Today's students demand more structure and have more difficulty with complex concepts. The issue is further complicated by the probability that faculty are more akin to traditional students than to the new students in their mode of learning. According to the authors, liberal learning is not beyond these new students in either their ability to grasp the education or their desire to pursue it. But facilitating that learning means a challenge for today's faculty. And, it means a much needed examination of the overall value of liberal education for the individual in both personal and practical terms.

Edwin Harwood calls for balance between personal development (so characteristic of liberal education) and professional/vocational training or the development of practical skills. This solution heralds a relatively easy problem. If we can construct out of a situation a seesaw, then we can define and organize the problem. In his essay, "Viva the Liberal Arts! Viva Specialization!" Harwood describes a conflict between two "cultures"—between that of the scholar-generalist and that of the vocational-specialist. In a seesaw construct, both "cultures" are important. This is not to be passed over lightly for in many discussions of liberal learning, the vocational-specialist has scant place. According to Harwood, "when we debunk the narrow engineering curriculum or any other line of vocational specialization, we risk our own and other societies' future well-being." He refers, of course, to our standard of living and the potential for addressing technologically the range of future social and economic ills.

On one end of our precarious balance sit the vocational-specialists; on the other, the scholar-generalists. How might a more enduring and dynamic equilibrium be achieved? It is in a blending of the two extremes, says the author. In the midsection of our metaphorical seesaw are already gathered the scholar-specialists—scholars who have selected a career of very narrow research. To this cluster Harwood adds a new breed, the vocational-generalist—a category of individuals who are technically proficient in some vocational skill but who have broad, extracurricular interests. "I feel the university must encourage amateur intellectual involvements that fall outside a chosen branch of study," Harwood suggests. The problem is "how to create [a liberal arts] ethic that will allow the university to merge specialized training with amateur pursuits." These two quotes suggest two possible avenues for exploration: (1) a rigid program of professional training and sufficient time to develop other interests; and (2) an effort to blend or merge technical training and the liberal arts. In either case a more durable and creative balance would be struck.

There is a third avenue which is simply that many "unblended" liberal arts courses are as suitable for a program of professional training as any that could be developed for a particular career track. According to Joseph Claxton, in his " 'Genuine' Education: An Excellent Preparation for Law School," the aims of liberal education "have direct relevance not just to legal education in a university setting, but to the application of that education to 'real world' problems experienced by attorneys." Liberal education provides opportunity for disciplined self-expression, a skill of great importance to lawyers. But skills are not everything. "What good is a professional life without philosophical insight or moral sensibilities?," Claxton asks. Such rhetorical questions do not defeat currently popular curricular designs like "prelaw" programs. The prelaw myth grew out of a desire to blend professional and liberal arts tracks at the undergraduate level, but the blend is, in effect, an undesirable compromise. A genuine liberal education, Claxton asserts, is an excellent preparation for law school (or any other professional school).

Thus the essays in this collection, in which members of the faculty of Mercer University offer their own reflections on the nature and purpose of liberal arts education, address the status and future of liberal education from a variety of contexts and perspectives. The authors—"pioneers" and "pallbearers" alike—have tried to clarify the ideals of liberal education before they have become preoccupied with the mundane considerations of implementation. This volume is offered in the hope that readers will find the discussions of liberal arts education in it refreshing and innocent.

Liberal Education and the Christian Intellectual Tradition

Willis B. Glover

Many highly intelligent and well-educated people in this country are deeply committed to what they call "liberal education." Yet there is little understanding of what the term "liberal education" means, and there are many dire predictions of its early demise. It is interesting that there has been so little effort to define just what kind of education it is that is still deemed appropriate for those entering the learned professions. If the values of liberal education are lost to this culture, it will not be from lack of money or from competition with other programs of study but because its proponents and practitioners have done such a poor job of understanding and explaining what it is. Even professors who are themselves committed to the liberal arts and sciences are for the most part content to describe liberal education in unexamined clichés. It is often defined as the education proper to free men. The definition is ancient and has some historical merit; but it is hardly helpful in a society in which all men are recognized to be free. In another genetic fallacy liberal education is said to be education that frees from ignorance and prejudice. Will Rogers once remarked that we are all ignorant, but of different things. All education frees from ignorance of some sort. Engineering, computer science, medicine, even less prestigious kinds of vocational training may be said to emancipate from ignorance. Freedom from prejudice is getting closer, but it would be more accurate to say that liberal education frees one from immoral prejudice. Freedom from bad prejudices involves the inculcation of what Burke called "just prejudice," that is, a commitment to values that gives us an adequately based preexisting orientation in situations that confront us unexpectedly. How well even the best liberal colleges are doing that is open to question. Certainly the values reflected in the strident opposition of Vassar students to having William Buckley speak on their campus in 1980 can hardly be called liberal.

Still another cliché is that liberal education teaches the student to think. The admissions programs of the very best liberal arts colleges suggest that the best candidates for admission are those who already know how to think and that the colleges are not very optimistic about teaching those who do not. It is true that liberal education disciplines the mind and sharpens the critical intelligence, but so do rigorous programs of study in engineering or business administration. (It may be remarked here that like other rigorous fields of study liberal education is inevitably elitist. This is not because of any desire to be exclusive, but simply because most people are not capable intellectually of a real liberal education. An elitist liberal arts college should generate no more moral outrage than the elitism of a school like the Massachusetts Institute of Technology or any good school of medicine.)

What is needed is an analysis that discovers the reason a certain kind of education called liberal—a kind of education that is not in obvious ways very practical—should in fact be so valuable. The distinctive thing about liberal education is that it broadens and deepens the context in which the critical intelligence is used because it organically relates various disciplines around the great problems of personal existence, the nature of the world, and the difficulties of human community. The task of the liberal college is to introduce the student to the heart of Western culture and so to help him achieve a sense of reality and value in terms of which he can relate his own career to the rich and varied life of the whole society. In the pluralistic, badly disintegrated culture of the modern world this is an immensely difficult task; but the situation that creates the difficulty gives the task a commensurate importance. The ends of liberal education cannot be accomplished by a straightforward analysis of Western civilization because such an analysis would have to be from some point of view with the result that the richness of the whole common effort of the West would be lost. Furthermore, the background for understanding such an analysis would be lacking. To provide that background is precisely what liberal education is about. The approach has to be indirect by acquaintance with some of the science, theology, philosophy, literature, and history that furnish insights into the basic commitments and patterns of ideas that constitute Western culture. No mind can grasp the whole of Western culture, and, therefore, no one combination of courses can be identified with liberal education. Certainly programs of general education that undertake to teach everyone a little superficial information about a variety of disciplines are no solution to the problem.

If liberal education is to furnish a solution, it must provide some different kind of common ground. It would seem that it does, in fact, in some significant degree do so. The argument here is based upon the assumption that at the root of every identifiable culture is some basic "sense of reality" or "mode of being aware of the world and of our experience in it" which is shared throughout the culture and finds expression in institutions and in a developing tradition. This basic orientation of experience is in any viable culture characteristic of uneducated as well as educated people. The purpose of liberal education is to achieve an intellectual grasp of what is basic in the culture so that a more intelligent and self-conscious participation in the common life will become possible. This is a process that cannot be confined to imparting information and stimulating ratiocination; liberal education is a participation in culture and an effort to penetrate through the culture in order to ground one's personal existence in the reality that the culture seeks to express. Vocational education and technical training are rightly considered "preparation for life"; the liberal arts and sciences ought not to be so considered. They are not preparation, but initiation, a deepening of participation in the life of the culture and an extension of human sympathies and awareness. Many students of liberal arts colleges will never be so alive again as they are during their student days of close contact with the best thought and art of the West.

This fact is, no doubt, an indictment of our culture and our education, but it ought to warn us against thinking of the liberal arts as a mere "preparation for life." That caveat made, it is necessary to add that people who have experienced this initiation are better equipped to deal with a wider range of situations, to see problems in a broader context, and to act intelligently when confronted with unanticipated problems and situations—an experience which is continually recurring in the dynamic culture of the West. In this sense liberal education does prepare for future developments. What appear to be our major problems now are not those we anticipated twenty, or even ten, years ago. Despite the confusion about it, liberal education is here to stay because of its value in orienting able people to the culture as a whole and through them orienting society with respect to its own past experience and system of values.

The interpretation of liberal education here presented is supported by the continuity of purpose and function which it has maintained through radical changes in curriculum. In modern times additions to the liberal curriculum of science, history, and modern literature were major changes; and they paved the way for the even more radical change of abandoning the study of classical culture as the core of the liberal arts. From the Middle Ages to about 1900, despite additions to the curriculum and shifts of emphasis from one classical writer to another, the study of the classics remained the essential ingredient of a liberal education. Another major part of the curriculum was an introduction to the Bible and to the theological tradition stemming from it. The latter was communicated in part through church and family; but in most colleges there was also some formal treatment of these subjects. In this century fewer and fewer liberal arts students have any instruction at all in Christian studies per se, and classical scholarship has become merely one specialized field among many in the liberal college—and not one that attracts many students. Yet the typical member of a late-twentieth-century liberal arts faculty, who has no Greek and little Latin, feels a strong sense of continuity with the liberal arts tradition of previous centuries. The explanation for this surprising sense of continuity through such radical changes in curriculum is not to be found in the curriculum as a list of disciplines, but rather in the function which these disciplines perform in orienting the student toward the culture as a whole. Greco-Roman civilization and the Judeo-Christian tradition are the two most important sources of the modern West. That is why they were so long capable of constituting the core of liberal education. This same function is now performed by courses in science, history, mathematics, modern literature, philosophy, and the behavioral sciences.

In this new mode liberal education still exists and is very important to our society; but something important has been left out. The blend of classical and Christian ethics that was the staple of liberal education from the Renaissance to our own century was never very sound, and it involved the adulteration of each of these great traditions with the other so that the edges of both were blunted. Nevertheless, this forced ethical fusion furnished an important dimension to the liberal arts tradition. Liberal education at its best transcends the merely intellectual; it needs to involve the student in some kind of personal commitment to values basic in his cultural tradition. In short, there is an inescapable religious dimension in the best liberal education just as there is an inescapable religious dimension in any live culture.

A major problem is that the religious situation in the last three centuries has been complicated and is not well understood even among the liberally educated. The history of Christian theology in this period is not obscure, but it is also not significant; or to be more accurate it is significant primarily in its failure to apprehend fully the Christian intellectual tradition and to have a decisive influence on the development of the intellectual culture of the West. The Christian intellectual tradition is, of course, much broader than the formal study of theology. With few exceptions its most outstanding figures in recent times are not professional theologians at all. Best known are literary figures: Dostoevski, Francois Mauriac, T. S. Eliot, Thornton Wilder, Tolkien, and so forth. But there are outstanding scholars also: Von Ranke, Lord Acton, C. S. Lewis, Douglas Bush, J. H. Hexter, and others; and philosophers: Michael Polanyi, Gabriel Marcel and maybe even Jaspers, and so forth.

Over against this continuing Christian tradition there have developed strong secular humanistic faiths that both complicate and obscure the religious and cultural situation. The classical tradition, however one may interpret its previous role, has ceased to be a major source of creative energy. The present situation is that of a dichotomy between Christianity and the secular faiths of modern humanism. It is the thesis of this paper that the two branches of this dichotomy have a common ground in the biblical-Christian tradition and that this common ground offers the opportunity for a more vigorous and perceptive approach to liberal education. The plausibility of this may become more evident upon consideration of some aspects of the development of Western intellectual culture since the late Middle Ages.

The conventional interpretation of the Renaissance is that it was the period in which European culture was secularized. There is one sense in which this is true. By the fifteenth century laymen were taking a much larger role in intellectual life. Even in this regard one should not overstate the case. Copernicus was a monk; and it would be hard to name anyone in the sixteenth century, unless perhaps Galileo, who has had a greater influence on subsequent intellectual history than Luther or Calvin. The significant question, however, is not whether laymen became more articulate in the Renaissance; the key issue is whether European culture in the fifteenth and sixteenth centuries was less Christian in its general content and orientation. Was this the time in which the modern secular alternative to Christianity arose? There is abundant evidence that it was not. The scholarship of the past two generations has shown that the basic orientation of the Renaissance humanists was Christian and that many of them, including Petrarch and Lorenzo Valla, were very pious men. On the question of the sinfulness of man Valla seems to have been much closer to Luther than to Erasmus, and, of course, Erasmus himself was a very sincere Christian. Among American scholars responsible for this radical change in interpretation, Oskar Kristeller, John Herman Randall, Jr., and Charles Trinkaus are particularly interesting because Kristeller is a Jew, Randall an atheist, and Trinkaus, according to the biographical sketch in *Contemporary Authors*, had Methodist parents but is himself religiously "inactive." In 1970 Trinkaus published a heavily documented, two-volume work on the basis for the famed Renaissance view of the dignity of man; it bears the interesting title *In Our Image and Likeness*, a title taken from the first chapter of Genesis. The thesis of Trinkaus's work is that the primary source for the exalted view of man in the Renaissance was the biblical doctrine of Creation; and the next most important source was the doctrine of the Incarnation. In the first chapter of Genesis the rest of the creation is turned over to man for him to "subdue" and "dominate." Man does not merely have a high place in the order of the cosmos; the Greeks had thought as much, though they had not accorded him the highest place. To the Renaissance humanists and Platonists, who were developing a biblical tradition and following certain of the ancient church fathers, man was much more. Made in the image of the transcendent God, man also transcended the rest of creation in his capacity to know God. It is interesting to see how this affected the neoplatonism of Pico; instead of assigning man to an intermediate position between matter and spirit Pico saw man as independent of the Great Chain of Being and capable of choosing any place along it or of transcending it altogether in his God-likeness.

The doctrine of the Incarnation was also a major source of the Renaissance view of man. Whereas medieval scholars were wont to emphasize the greatness of God's love that He would stoop so low as to become man, the humanists pointed out that man was so great that God could become man.

The thesis of Trinkaus is, of course, too radical a change to have gone uncontroverted. John H. Geerken, for example, in a long review in *The Journal of the History of Philosophy* (1974) argues that Trinkaus does not sufficiently consider the heroic ideal and its incompatibility with Christian ethics. Criticism and qualification were to be expected; but Trinkaus's documentation is very thorough, his thesis is supported by the previous works of very able Renaissance scholars, and it has already won a following large enough to make it probable that it will very soon be the consensus of Renaissance scholarship. A full generation before Trinkaus published *In Our Image and Likeness*, Paul Hazard had pointed out in what is now a classic of historical scholarship when the secularization of Western culture really began. His *La Crise de la conscience européene* (English translation: *The European Mind*, 1680-1715) indicates that in a single generation, for the first time in European history, a substantial number of the intellectual leaders of Europe repudiated Christianity and took a stand on other ground. This was the beginning of the Enlightenment at the end of the seventeenth century.

One must be careful in using such a phrase as "the Enlightenment view of man." For one thing many important figures in the eighteenth century can hardly be called "Enlightened" at all. Consider Robert Walpole, or the Jansenists, or Isaac Watts, or Wesley. Judged by his influence on subsequent history, Wesley was at least as significant a figure as Voltaire or Robespierre—though, it must be admitted, not as significant as Rousseau. Another difficulty is that many who called themselves Christians were further from traditional Christian belief than many who called themselves deists. Nevertheless, it is possible to make some general comments on the new humanistic faith of the Enlightenment. The Renaissance had continued the development of biblical anthropology; in the Enlightenment this biblical view of man was secularized. The Enlightenment understanding of man as an historical being, responsible for his own future, operating without limitation on the dead and purposeless world of modern science, even the concept of his "perfectibility" are derivatives from the biblical-Christian tradition. Secularization did, of course, produce radical changes in this tradition. Deism effectively removed God from history; He was relegated to a past act of creation and a future act of judgment. Man was thus left the only being actively purposeful in history. He was in the Enlightenment free of any limitation by God's will except insofar as that was incorporated in the "Laws of Nature." When deism died out at the end of the century (except that it continued on as a popular, residual kind of Christian heresy), modern, atheistic man felt himself freer than ever. His God-like freedom has been sometimes exhilarating, sometimes terrifying; but, however experienced, it is the peculiar result of the biblical tradition turned atheistic.

One way of understanding the Enlightenment is that it was a declaration of emancipation from God. It is true that few in the eighteenth century would have put it that way; neither Christians nor deists were consciously in such rebellion. Nevertheless, the repudiation of original sin amounted to an assumption of moral independence. Belief in the fundamental goodness of man was not an empirical judgment but an act of faith. In Voltaire's *Candide* the only person not either a fool or a charlatan is an anabaptist who is thrown to the sharks soon after his introduction; yet Voltaire fervently believed in the goodness of man and wrote several arguments against Pascal's more realistic anthropology.

With the eclipse of deism and the differentiation of the new humanism into the deification of various historical causes or communities, some of these things became more obvious; but an adequate analysis of the religious situation in the modern West has yet to be made. There is not space here to discuss the various differentiated, non-Christian, humanistic faiths. The first was the Jacobin movement of the French Revolution. Then there was scientific humanism with its first major exponent in Saint-Simon. Various socialisms and nationalisms followed, Marxism being by far the most significant politically. The original, undifferentiated Enlightenment faith continued in what Eric Voegelin calls Progressivism.

The situation that we now face is a fundamental dichotomy between Christianity and various forms of atheistic humanism. The differences between the two faiths are the source of much confusion in modern culture. For example, are democratic societies founded on the belief that men are so prone to the misuse of power that none can be trusted with it unless controlled by others; or is democracy based on the idea that men are basically good and that the occasional wickedness of individual men will be swallowed up in the general goodness of the common man? A better understanding of these fundamental disagreements in the bases of our culture would diminish some of our confusions and facilitate the discovery of some generally acceptable approach to the injustices that all recognize.

The disagreements between Christianity and modern humanism are, however, less significant for the development of liberal education than what these faiths have in common. The common ground between them is so great as to justify calling atheistic humanism a fourth biblical religion after Judaism, Christianity, and Islam. The purposeful world and the explanations of physical phenomena in terms of teleologies inherent in things are gone. For modern humanism the contingent world of the biblical tradition is no longer contingent because the transcendent God is no longer recognized; but it remains the "dead," purposeless world of modern physics in which things are acted upon instead of acting through some inherent tendency. This orientation to the world was a derivative of the biblical doctrine of creation. The relevance of Christian theology to science was first clearly seen in the early fourteenth century. Ernest Moody put the matter succinctly; for the fourteenth-century scholar, he says:

> The eternal, necessary and predictable natural world of Aristotle had been replaced by the created, contingent, and only conditionally predictable natural order compatible with Christian Faith ["Ockham, Buridan, and Nicholas of Autrecourt," *Franciscan Studies* 7 (1947): 142].

More important was the continuation in the Enlightenment and later of an essentially biblical anthropology, albeit radically modified by the absence of any relationship to God and consequently by the absence of the biblical concept of sin. Man was still the transcendently free, historical being of the creation story. The world was his to understand, dominate, and use.

The significant thing and the thing that has been too much over-looked is that the structure of the Western mind, both Christian and humanistic, is founded primarily in the biblical-Christian tradition. Recognition of this fact is essential to establishing liberal education on a secure foundation. Understanding the basic orientations toward experience that make Western civilization what it is will enable us to direct the future development of liberal education in rational and cumulative ways. To make such an understanding current even in the limited circles of academia will not be easy. Secular humanism fought hard to achieve its emancipation from Christianity. One of the main tactics in this fight was condescension toward the Christian faith as an obsolete superstition hanging on in popular circles. This has been and still is a serious obstacle to an accurate appraisal of the role of Christian faith in the development of Western culture. But the emancipation is now enough complete, especially in the free West that a frank approach to intellectual history ought to be possible. (Paradoxically, the totalitarian countries are more afraid of Christianity than humanists in the democratic West.)

In this situation the Christian scholar and the Christian college need to reappropriate their own intellectual tradition. In the words of Stanley Hopper there is a need to rethink our history possessively. The present stage of historical scholarship makes this an exciting prospect. In the liberal college this prospect ought to be pursued in a manner that increases mutual understanding among various faiths and not in an aggressive spirit. Christians know that the roots of their faith are predominantly in Judaism, but few are tempted to become Jews. Secular humanists by analogy should be able to discover the roots of their faith in the biblical-Christian tradition without being threatened in the position to which they are committed.

It is generally accepted that the two major sources of the Western tradition are Greco-Roman and Hebrew-Christian. From the early eighteenth century until recently, however, appreciation of the latter influence has been too much restricted to literary traditions and to some degree of humanitarian morality. It is only in this century that the depth of the biblical influence is beginning to be understood. Significant examples from recent studies in intellectual history are easily found. It is common knowledge that the first modern existential-ist was the Christian Søren Kierkegaard. His roots, moreover, go back to Pascal, and ultimately to Saint Augustine and the New Testament. Existentialism has, of course, other sources—Nietzsche, for example, and Husserl—but this whole philosophical orientation is the develop-ment of an essentially biblical view of man as radically free, a historical being producing his own future by the exercise of his will. Nietzsche liked to think of himself as reviving a "Dionysian" element of classical thought, but as has been often remarked, it is hard to imagine Nietzsche apart from the background of Christian culture.

In the English-speaking world the most prominent current philos-ophy is called analytical. Analytical philosophy with its emphasis on language analysis developed out of logical positivism, which has its roots in an empirical tradition that goes back through Hume and Berkeley and Hobbes to the Christian nominalists of the fourteenth century, of whom William of Ockham is the most famous. Ernest Moody published an article in the *Philosophical Review* in 1958 entitled "Empiricism and Metaphysics in Medieval Philosophy." In this article he argues that the mainstream of modern philosophy has been radically different from the mainstream of Greek philosophy. The latter was "rationalistic and speculative"; modern philosophy is "empirical and critical." By "critical" he refers to the emphasis of modern philosophy on epistemology as distinct from the ancient emphasis on metaphysics. Professor Moody credits this difference to the impact of late medieval theology, especially the nominalist concern with the implications of the doctrine of Creation.

Every major philosophy of the modern world has roots in the biblical-Christian tradition. The process philosophers—Hegel, Berg-son, Whitehead—are clearly indebted to the sense of reality as histori-cal that stems from the biblical tradition. Also, the voluntarism that characterized the medieval nominalists and is prominent in so many modern philosophies is biblical-Christian in origin. On the strength of his emphasis on will and artifice Michael Oakeshott calls Hobbes an Augustinian. (See also the present writer's "Human Nature and the State in Hobbes," *Journal of the History of Philosophy* 4 [1966]: 310-11). Not only is voluntarism an important element in Bergson, Whitehead, Husserl, and the existentialists; we find Hume saying "reason is and ought to be the slave of the passions."

Even better documented is the role of Christian theology, especially the doctrine of Creation, in the origins of modern science. Hellenistic science stagnated in the second century B.C. Moslem science, after flourishing for a brief period, also stagnated. The epistemological breakthrough that opened the way to modern science was first recognized to be a product of the doctrine of Creation by Pierre Duhem early in this century. Duhem may have somewhat overstated his case; but his discovery is now generally accepted. Although he makes no reference to the historical work of Duhem, Michael Foster published articles in *Mind* in the 1930s which showed that significant affinities exist between Christian theology and modern science. Owen Barfield's brilliant treatise, *Saving the Appearances* (1965?), even argues that if we take the nature of science seriously it will lead us back to a recognition of Creation!

The Christian origin of the famed Renaissance view of man was mentioned above. The significant thing to note is that it is precisely this Christian anthropology that has been secularized into modern atheistic humanism. The Enlightenment, far from being a return to classical paganism, was an affirmation of the transcendent, historical man of Christian tradition declaring his emancipation from God and his capacity to perfect himself and his society.

The peculiarly Western sense of history with its strong orientation toward the future and its sometimes overwhelming sense of responsibility for that future originates in the biblical tradition. (Excellent brief statements of this are found in J. H. Hexter, *The Judaeo-Christian Tradition,* and Mircea Eliade, *Cosmos and History.* Fuller discussions are included in Eric Voegelin, *Israel and Revelation,* and in any number of recent theological and biblical studies. Gerhard von Rad's *Theology of the Old Testament* and Jurgen Moltmann's *Theology of Hope* come readily to mind.) The biblical conception of history as a process in which the redemptive purposes of God move in a unidirectional manner toward culmination in a "new creation" was converted in the Enlightenment into a more mundane conception of progress. Recent controversy over whether the Greeks had any sense of progress has produced no evidence that the limited idea of a progress in knowledge that some Greeks had was anything like the dominating conception of the modern world. The shadow image of the modern belief in progress, or at least in its possibility, is the fear of impending doom resulting from man's failure to be equal to his historical responsibilities. Modern man vacillates between too optimistic a view of his possibilities and despair over his moral weakness.

So commonplace as to be easily overlooked is the unique emphasis on historical scholarship that has characterized recent Western culture. It is under Western influence since about 1800 that the histories of other cultures have been written. Neither the Greeks nor the Romans nor any other people, except when influenced by modern Westerners, have developed a serious scholarship concerning their own origins. It is a question why this interest in history, which is so obviously suggested by the Hebrew-Christian tradition, should have been so slow developing. The problem is complex, but undoubtedly the dominance of Aristotle in the methodology of the Middle Ages, the Renaissance tendency to use the ancient historians as models, and the eighteenth-century belief in unchanging laws of nature as the fundamental reality inhibited the development of the dynamic, historical conception of reality presented in the Bible. Even Hume, certainly no naive mechanist, said in his *Inquiry*:

> Mankind are so much the same, in all times and places, that history informs us of nothing new or strange in this particular. Its chief use is only to discover the constant and universal principles of human nature by showing men in all varieties of circumstances and situations.

This was the approach to history of the great Greek and Roman historians; but it is not the attitude that made the nineteenth century the "age of history."

The influence of the biblical tradition on literature has been mentioned and requires no elaboration. In our own age, when secularism is stronger than ever before, that influence shows little or no sign of abating. One has only to recall the names of T. S. Eliot, W. H. Auden, Flannery O'Connor, William Faulkner, Vladimir Volkoff, and many others.

This statement has dealt mostly with the obvious and well-established; yet the fundamental role of the biblical-Christian tradition in the development of our culture has been systematically neglected except by a few specialists. This is surely the main reason Western culture and the liberal education that reflects it is in a state of chaotic disintegration. Whatever one's religious commitment, he can hardly hope to orient himself realistically in today's world if he fails to take seriously the tradition that more than any other has provided the framework of Western intellectual history.

If the point of this essay has been made, it must be realized that not only Christians but secular humanists of many varieties are heirs of the biblical-Christian tradition. Various prejudices will make it hard for many humanists to accept this; but the demands of our cultural situation make it imperative that they try to do so in order that there can be achieved a deeper and more integrative understanding of the culture which now, for better or for worse, dominates the globe as no other has ever done.

As for Christian scholars, they have little reason for pride or boasting. With few exceptions Christian theology since the beginning of the Enlightenment has been a disaster area. The ablest Christian leadership has for the most part either been irrelevant to the important developments in modern culture or has been so diffident in the face of secular science and scholarship that it has lost its grasp on its own tradition and any significant influence on intellectual history. This judgment is, of course, restricted to the professional Christian leadership including theologians. As has been abundantly illustrated, the great tradition itself lives on in the culture, albeit in great part anonymously. Another reason Christians have ground for some humility is that this Western civilization, which more than any other can be described as Christian, has produced so much that one can hardly be proud of. Enough has been said on that subject in other places; suffice it to say here that at least the Christian doctrine of sin offers an explanation of the paradox.

The scholarship of the past few decades in a number of fields presents the liberal arts college with an unprecedented opportunity. There is no reason that this opportunity cannot be seized by secular colleges dominated by non-Christian humanists. Since so many of the very best colleges can be so decribed, it is, indeed, likely that the revival of liberal education along the lines suggested in this essay may occur first in secular institutions. That may be the healthiest development possible. Throughout Christian history there has been a tendency for Christians to identify the cultural products of Christian faith with the faith itself. From a Christian point of view this is a very grievous error. Any faith widely held throughout a human society will generate culture. But no matter how much the earthly city may be affected by ideas and orientations stemming out of the biblical revelation, it cannot transform itself into the City of God. No doubt Christians for the general good ought to hold up the community of the City of God as a model for the reform of the earthly city; but such reforms can never produce the City of God. As a matter of historical fact there is a sense in which Western civilization is Christian. It is, however, very dangerous to use this fact apologetically, for it is more likely to produce an arrogant idolatry than a bulwark of faith.

In this situation Christians must continue as in the past to wrestle with the subtle problems and temptations in the relation of faith to culture. The intent of this essay is not apologetic nor evangelistic. It is concerned with the revitalization of liberal education. All caveats having been made, however, the opportunity which recent historical scholarship offers the Christian liberal arts college is obvious. If a Christian college with intelligent leadership should undertake to move in the direction here indicated with intellectual honesty and openness to contrary opinions and commitments, it might initiate a very significant movement, not only in education, but in the intellectual history of the West.

Epilogue

How can a particular Christian college take advantage of the opportunity for Christian education offered by the present state of scholarship? For one, the college can practice a sophisticated selectivity in choosing faculty members who are alive to or at least open to the relevance of recent scholarship to the development of Christian education at the college level. The college administration could also use its resources for outside speakers and visiting faculty members so as continually to stimulate students and faculty to think about the relationship of faith to learning. The astonishing possibilities cannot be realized by curriculum revision, however radical, but only by committed scholars and honest scholarship.

Science as a
Liberal Arts Discipline

Dan R. Quisenberry

The Method of Science

A useful working definition of science is that it is a method for describing, creating, and understanding human experience. But first, the significance of the indefinite article *a* that precedes the word *method* must be emphasized. There are many ways of dealing with human experience, including, for example, the arts of music, poetry, painting, and drama. Science is only one way, albeit a very powerful one. Science, therefore, is a rather specialized view of experience, and this must be kept in mind in the subsequent discussions of some of the arbitrariness associated with it.

The Nature of Human Experience. Experience in the context in which we shall use it is the sum total of everything that happens to us during our waking, and perhaps even sleeping, hours, along with the reflections on these happenings made by our minds. These happenings are given various terms—sense impressions, sensations, sensory perceptions—by philosophers and psychologists. Put more specifically, we as individuals are continually seeing, hearing, touching, tasting, and smelling, and from our mental reactions to these sensations are creating ideas about the objects of our perception and their relations to each other. (This is a simplification of a very difficult philosophical problem, about which reams of philosophical literature have been written.) Before the term experience becomes meaningful in the context in which we use it, it is necessary to postulate also that the sense impressions of different individuals agree sufficiently so that the individuals can discuss their impressions without hopeless confusion. If A could not act on the presumption that B's normal experiences in the same environment as A closely approximate A's, there could be no science. Of course, sometimes the experience of A will differ radically from that of B, because the perceptions of A or B are "abnormal." In practice, however, distinctions between normal and abnormal experience have been fairly easily established.

Not all human experience has been incorporated into science. Still, the domain of experience tackled by science is continually expanding and cannot be defined too closely. For instance, while it has been customary to take for granted that physics has nothing to do with the observed behavior of living things, scientists nowadays have no hesitation in developing biophysics and psychophysics, in which the methods of physics are applied directly to biology and psychology. Similarly, although experience connected with the transformation of one substance into another has historically been considered the province of the chemist rather than the physicist, the field of chemical physics is now flourishing, and the distinction between chemistry and physics, except for artificial administrative purposes, has become practically negligible. To attempt to delimit the domain of experience peculiar to science here would be to place the emphasis in the wrong place. It is the method of science that is important.

Description in Science. The word description literally means a writing about something. It can also be used in the sense of talking about the thing being described, with the intention that the listener form some idea of it without actually seeing it himself. Description requires that the talker should, by comparison with other things alike or different, create in the mind of the listener an image of the thing described. In science, to describe experience is to talk about things observed in the talker's environment; but in science the talking is governed by the rather stringent limitation that it must relate to the search for order in experience. The flux of experience as encountered by a young child must be a rather chaotic affair, and presumably the same was true of man in the early stages of his development. But gradually certain patterns emerged in the form of such repetitive natural phenomena as the succession of day and night, and the courses of the stars across the heavens. These gave man a handle on his experience; he could build a feeling of confidence in the light of this observed order, even when it was occasionally marred by disturbances like eclipses, violent storms, volcanic eruptions, or earthquakes. The perception of experience as involving a degree of order or regularity triumphed over the more pessimistic view that one could never feel any assurance about what was going to happen next. The victory of the optimistic point of view has made all science possible.

It is not only the common repetitive phenomena that seem to indicate order in human experience. Simple relations between apparently diverse experiences—between lightning and thunder, dark skies and rain or snow, the stretch of the bowstring and the speed of the arrow, the pitch of a musical note and the size of the struck object producing it, the rays of light reflected from a mirror and the size and shape of the mirror—all these relations suggest regularity in experience and stimulate the search for further examples. The curiosity thus developed has been one of the great driving forces of science and has led to the quest for relations of a more recondite kind—like those between electrical phenomena and magnetism; the size, shape, and constitution of solid objects and the ability to conduct electricity; and the velocity of light and the nature of the medium through which it is traveling.

When the properties that appear always to be related in a regular fashion can be specified with some degree of definiteness, it becomes possible to express the relation in precise language. Of course it will scarcely be worthwhile to do this unless the relation has been observed many times by many people in many different places, and general agreement has been reached about its nature. Under these circumstances the description of the relation becomes a physical law—a brief expression of a routine of human experience in the physical domain. So we have laws like Boyle's law for gases, Hooke's law for elastic substances, Ohm's law for electric currents, the law of refraction of light, and the law of the pendulum. In the establishment and enunciation of laws of this kind, sophistication of a high order is involved.

The very use of the term law conjures up in the mind of the average thoughtful person the vision of a law-abiding universe that it is the obligation of the scientist to discover or, perhaps more properly, to uncover bit by bit. From this standpoint, a physical law describes a regularity in experience ordained, as it were, from the beginning, but concealed from man until clever observers and experimenters came along and detected it. It must be stressed, however, that this is by no means the scientist's interpretation of law. To him it means no more and no less than the simplest possible description of a routine of experience, amply attested by numerous experimental tests under carefully controlled conditions. That there can be no element of logical necessity in its status is made clear by the fact that no physical law as yet set up has proved to be valid over the whole experimental range of the quantities to which it relates. Boyle's law, for example, ceases to be an accurate description of the behavior of a gas at very low temperatures. Under these circumstances, of course, all gases change their state, and near the transition point between phases Boyle's law no longer functions.

No law should ever be stated without an accompanying statement of its limits of application. The scientist seeks to establish laws that have the widest possible domain of applicability. At certain stages in the development of the science it was fondly hoped that more and more precise observation and more skillful selection of the variables influencing the observed behavior of systems would lead to laws of simple form. Newton, for example, had a profound confidence in the essential simplicity of nature. Unfortunately, experience indicates that this confidence was not well founded, though much depends on what is meant by simplicity.

Since a law states a relation connecting ideas that refer to experience, it is clear that a law's logical status cannot profitably be analyzed before settling the question of how these ideas are actually expressed in terms of experimental data. It is necessary, in other words, to examine the nature of physical concepts and their linguistic representation in order to understand how a law describes experience. Without such an analysis words like *pressure, electrical current*, and *mass*, and statements about them are meaningless. The purely operational significance of concepts must be contrasted with their theoretical meaning—their relation with other concepts in the same or related domains. The view, sometimes known as *operationalism*, that physical ideas have no validity unless they are definitely tied to specific operations in the laboratory must be examined with some thoroughness, as must the effect of this view on the development of theoretical science. Finally, law and theory are inextricably related to one another, for in every law there is an inevitable element of hypothesis.

The Creation of Experience in Science. The experience that is described in science should not be understood only as something taken in passively by the human observer, though that, indeed, is presumably how science started. People simply looked about them, tried to reckon with what they experienced as best they could, and accidentally came upon signs of order. But man eventually woke up to the fact that the experience received in this way is limited in extent and made the overwhelmingly important discovery that man himself can create experience by setting up arbitrary arrangements of objects and performing operations on them with the aim of seeing what will happen. Archimedes, for instance, carried out an experiment when, instead of simply observing that some objects float in water and others do not, he tried to find out whether there is a relation between the weight of a given object in comparison with its size and the volume of water it displaces.

Experimentation is often referred to as controlled sense perception. This conveys some of the meaning of the process but misses its most vital characteristic—the fact that it produces experience new to man. In this sense experimentation may be described as the creation of experience. Science as a method became powerful when scientists decided not to limit experience only to what is at hand but to go out and produce it.

It is obvious even to a casual observer that experimentation is not a random affair, that scientists do not merely put things together in a haphazard way in the hope that something will emerge. The creation of experience in science is, in fact, based on prior experience, as well as on a considerable amount of reflection on that experience. But there are also psychological factors inherent in the inventiveness of man (and experiment certainly implies invention) that are not clearly understood.

To carry out an experiment a scientist abstracts from the totality of experience a certain small segment for special study. The question to be answered generally suggests a program, based on prior knowledge acquired in other situations. So a plan is devised, and appropriate equipment is chosen. The plan involves a program of operations to be carried out with the equipment. It is important to realize that this has to be in the mind of the experimenter before he can take any meaningful practical step. The final act is to perform the actual operations and to record the results in some suitable symbolic fashion. But this is not really the end after all, since the results are of no significance unless they have really created some new experience, and this can only be ascertained by examining and interpreting the results, and comparing them with the results of other persons who may have carried out experiments along the same line. Every step in the process calls for logical analysis.

Most physical experiments involve the measurement of a physical quantity. Put qualitatively and with deceptive simplicity, a measurement is an experiment or group of experiments whose aim is not merely to answer the question of how, but also that of how much. It represents the attempt to satisfy the quantitative urge by attaching numbers to the results of an experiment. Number is one of the most powerful and at the same time most mysterious concepts ever created by the human mind. Its origin is presumably to be found in early man's preoccupation with the comparison of assemblages of things as well as his later drive to order things with respect to variation in physical properties—as, for example, when he sought to make more specific his assertion that one thing is larger than another.

Essentially all measurement in science reduces to counting. But counting, except in the simple case of enumerating an assembly of entities, involves the use of a scale—a suitable physical surface on which a set of marks is inscribed in some arbitrary though definite fashion. A meter stick is a familiar illustration; others are a common thermometer, the speedometer of an automobile, or the face of a watch or clock. To use a scale for measurement a coincidence must be established between a mark on the scale and some physical object, such as a pointer. Most common physical measuring devices have built-in pointers. Thus that very simple but profoundly important instrument, the clock, has the hands as its pointers, whose coincidence with the marks on the face (the scale) by some arbitrarily chosen scheme, enables us to "tell" the time—to carry out the process of measuring time in any experiment. Another example of a measuring instrument is an electric ammeter, in which a needle is arranged so as to move across a scale, thereby attaching a number to the electric current flowing through the circuit in which the meter is inserted. All physical measurements involve some kind of pointer-readings.

A measurement determines the magnitude of a physical quantity. It is therefore essential to devise some way of identifying and talking about this quantity. This involves the notion of symbolism. A measurement could of course be described in purely operational terms, by stating that in a given case, when certain equipment was put together with a scale and pointer incorporated in it, certain readings were obtained when certain conditions were varied while others were held constant. This would describe what took place, but scientists have long since ceased to be satisfied with this way of describing the situation. To talk effectively about what has been done in the performance of an experimental measurement, it is advisable to replace the long-winded method described above by saying that the given set of operations constitutes a measurement of velocity, or mass, or pressure, or temperature, and so forth. As soon as we have introduced such terms we have embarked on what is called a symbolic terminology of science. The use of symbolism, whereby a single word or term stands for a whole series of operations, is obviously of the greatest importance in science. It brings us face to face with the use of mathematics in a more significant way than the mere employment of numbers does. This is because symbolic terms like velocity and temperature and pressure are ultimately represented by algebraic quantities that can figure in equations and be subject to the rules of mathematical manipulations.

Some humanists resent the general idea of the creation of experience in science. They feel that it distorts the natural world it is the duty of the scientist to study and report on. But the creation of experience is what constitutes the coming to grips with the world as the scientist conceives of it, and it must be remembered that humanists also create experience after their fashion. Nevertheless, criticism of the creation of experience can serve a useful purpose, if it encourages scientists to examine from the pragmatic standpoint what limits, if any, should be placed on the domain of physical experience. There does not appear, however, to be any aspect of human experience that is logically completely immune from examination by the scientist.

Understanding in Science. Scientists describe experience, they create experience by performing experiments, and having accomplished these essentials, they seek further to enlarge experience by understanding what they have done. To a scientist, understanding experience involved the development of appropriate theory. A theory is an imaginative construction of the mind that employs ideas suggested by experience and also by arbitrary notions whose origin it is difficult to trace; together these ideas and notions form a kind of mental picture of things as they might be. If a theory is to be of any use, it must be possible in reasonably unambiguous fashion to draw consequences from it that can be identified with actual experience. If it is really to be successful the theory must predict results that have not previously been experienced; the suggested experimentation when performed must then substantiate the prediction.

The history of science is filled with examples of successful prediction of new experience by theories. One thinks, for instance, of the prediction of the red shift in spectral lines in an intense gravitational field like that of the sun, as predicted by Einstein's general theory of relativity. Still more famous and indeed awe-inspiring in its ultimate impact on technology is Einstein's prediction of the relation between mass and energy ($E=mc^2$), based on his special theory of relativity. Great intellectual power is inherent in the predictive capacity of a successful theory and such theories play a vital role in the creation of new experience.

An emphasis on predictive ability as the criterion for success oversimplifies the appraisal of new theories. If successful prediction were the sole criterion, theorizing might well be reduced to a gambling game in which a lucky guess wins the prize. Moreover, it may be asked, what is to be done if two quite different theories predict the same result, and the prediction is verified? Could the scientist be satisfied with this situation? The answer is that theories must be appraised on other bases as well. Among these bases are judgments on the choice of concepts or constructs acceptable in terms of known experience; the limitation in the number of independent constructs employed; the mathematical elegance and rigor in the formulation of the theory; and the comprehensiveness of the theory—the extent of the domain of experience in which it works. All these judgments play a role in any valid appraisal of the contribution of a theory to the understanding of experience.

The Logical Structure of Physical Theory

Analysis. Having discussed the nature of science and emphasized the significance of physical law, experiment, and theory, we now find it necessary to examine in greater detail the nature of a theory, for it is the key to understanding all science.

There are two fundamental approaches we can take, the psychological and the logical. The first would investigate how clever people come to create theories. This may properly be called part of the psychology of science. It is a very difficult subject, and it is therefore not surprising that its exploration has led to little of positive value. One might suppose that creative scientists would have been at pains to indicate at some length how they arrived at the basis of their theories, but they have not often done so, or at any rate not in such fashion as to provide definite recipes for the construction of theories. Jacques Hadamard has presented interesting illustrations of mathematical discoveries by Jules Henri Poincare and others, but it must be confessed that from any practical standpoint the results are disappointing.[1] The same is true of the more recent ambitious attempts by Abraham Moles and Rene Leclercq.[2] There are hints, but a much more thoroughgoing psychological investigation is needed.

Here we shall take the second approach and make a logical analysis of physical theory and try to grasp the significance of its various components and their relation to each other. While this will of course not provide a recipe for the concoction of theories, it will set forth the structure of a theory in such a manner that we can more readily understand the various questions of a methodological nature that may appropriately be raised about physical theories in every field of science. It should give us a pretty good notion of what scientists mean when they say that theory provides an understanding of a part of human experience.

For convenience, a physical theory can be logically analyzed in terms of the following schema:

1. Primitive, intuitive notions

---

[1] J. Hadamand, *An Essay on the Psychology of Invention in the Mathematical Fields* (Princeton NJ: Princeton University Press, 1945).

[2] A. Moles, *La Creation scientifique* (Geneva: Editions Rene Kister, 1957); R. Leclercq, *Traite de la methode scientifique* (Paris: Dunod, 1965).

2. More precisely defined constructs

3. Postulates or hypotheses connecting the constructs

4. Deduced laws

5. Experimental testing of the deductions.

Let us try to make this schema clear. The best we can do in the way of grasping the meaning of anything is to talk about it in words that compare it with something supposedly more familiar. Thus we seek to, for example, understand light in terms of waves, and the picture that the mind conjures up is one of waves on the surface of water-waves as a visual experience. To get a clear idea of even a surface water-wave, however, implies our ability to recognize motion as the displacement of something through space as time goes on. Now time and space are primitive and rather ill-defined notions that are nevertheless fundamental for physical theorizing. One cannot do business without them. But the creative physicist generally takes them for granted. He thinks that every intelligent person will be willing to admit a familiarity with the concepts of space and time, and so in building theories the creative physicist does not hesitate to introduce such primitive notions as purely intuitive and not subject to further question. These constitute the first class in the preceding logical schema. Some other illustrations are the concept of a material particle, the concept of a field as a region in which each point is characterized by a definite value of some physical quantity (gravitational force, for instance), the idea of causality, the concept of probability that is so useful in statistical theories, and the notion of symmetry.

It is obvious that though these ideas are usually taken for granted by the framer of a physical theory they necessarily pose many serious problems for the philosopher of science, who looks with suspicion on too many undefined terms in any logical structure. At the same time even the philosopher has to admit that definition of anything ultimately means talking about it in terms of other things and that sooner or later one runs into undefined terms. Any dictionary illustrates this difficulty: all definitions reduce to circular definitions, as must be the case in any finite domain of human discourse. Euclid effectively recognized this difficulty with such undefined terms in his geometry as point, line, and plane. The definitions of these concepts, such as "a point is that which has no parts," are really no more than reminders that the concept ought to be pictured intuitively. In no branch of science can we ever get away from this fundamental difficulty: it faces the human race whenever the attempt is made to talk in terms of ideas instead of mere objects that can be pointed to.

Constructs and Symbolism. Using the primitive, intuitive concepts just discussed, the scientist proceeds to manufacture more precise concepts or "constructs," to use a term popularized by Henry Margenau that emphasizes more clearly what is meant.[3] There are at least two aspects of the question that demand more careful examination. These are the use of symbolism in the formation of constructs and the distinction between the operational and theoretical aspects of definition.

A symbol is a sign used to represent an object, an idea, or a situation. Thus a name symbolically designates a person or thing. But it can also represent an idea like love, or justice, or mass, or energy. All the terms in a dictionary are essentially symbols in the language in question. For reasons of economy, it is often customary, particularly in a science like physics, to replace actual linguistic names by single letters, as m for mass, V for volume, or p for pressure. The further and even more significant advantage of this is that if the thing being symbolically represented has a quantitative aspect and is therefore measurable, the symbol can take on numerical values and enter into mathematical relations with similar symbols. One can then apply all the paraphernalia of mathematics to it. This is a very powerful and revealing procedure. It enables us to express the content of physical laws in mathematical form, which is not just a matter of economy but also allows the use of mathematical manipulation in the deduction of new consequences from any statements in which the symbols enter.

A particularly important point emerges when the construct we are trying to define is a quantity to which a number may be attached, like mass, volume, or pressure. An electron, on the other hand, is not a quantity, and yet it is a perfectly good example of a construct. No number may be attached to it in itself, though its various properties— size, mass, charge, and velocity—are all quantitative under certain circumstances. In fact, it is hard to think of a physical construct that is not somehow concerned with numerical significance.

The assignment of a number to a construct or to a property of a

---

[3] H. Margenau, *The Nature of Physical Reality* (New York: McGraw-Hill, 1950).

construct involves what is called a measurement. This is a series of operations like those associated with any physical experiment, but with the added requirement that the equipment contain a scale and a pointer. The process of measurement is one with which nearly everyone is familiar, since all persons in countries of any pretense at all to civilization use it daily. In most cases the pointer is an actual solid moving indicator like a needle; but it does not have to be. Thus in an ordinary mercury-in-glass thermometer the pointer is the surface of the mercury column. Its coincidence with a mark on the scale is a measure of the temperature of the environment in which the thermometer is placed. The varieties of meters for the measurement of quantities like voltage, current, resistance, stress, pressure, speed, or intensity (of light or sound) are legion, but they all involve a pointer and a scale.

The definition of a physical construct that represents a quantity must provide directions as to how the quantity is to be measured. Every physical construct that represents a physical quantity subject to measurement must contain both epistemic and constitutive aspects in its definition. It is true that certain physical theories contain constructs representing quantities not subject to direct measurement. Such a construct might be the radius of an electron orbit in the simple Bohr model of an atom. Since there is no direct laboratory experiment by which this quantity can be measured, its definition will be entirely in terms of other quantities in the Bohr theory and hence wholly constitutive in character. In general, the more elaborate and sophisticated a theory is, the more purely constitutively defined constructs it will contain. Of course, these quantities must disappear in the laboratory equations resulting from the theory.

Postulates. The next step in the logical schema of a physical theory is the nature and place in the picture of the fundamental postulates. We have already looked at the general problem of the invention of clever ideas in the form of pictures of experience as it might be—pictures that, if accurate, are representations of actual experience in the observable world. But it is important to reemphasize the key position of hypotheses in physical theory. The very manufacture of constructs as discussed in the preceding section involves hypothesis. But from the standpoint of the logical structure of a theory it is customary to place special stress on the assumed relations among the constructs from which deductions can be made. Thus in the theory of mechanics in the version commonly associated with the name of Sir Isaac Newton the equation of motion (F=ma) is the key hypothesis. If we assume that it has universal validity, we can by appropriate choice of the force function F derive equations that directly describe types of motion encountered in our experience. One such equation is the famous law of freely falling bodies, where the force is that due to gravity.

A theory is of little value unless it leads to many consequences that are then shown to be in agreement with observation. A single set of fundamental postulates often manages to imply a host of consequences not immediately apparent from a casual inspection, but which can be developed with the use of a little imagination plus the use of appropriate mathematical analysis. This is the challenge of a plausible theory—to squeeze out of it as much as one can. This squeezing process can have two consequences. Either every deduction from a theory will be found to agree with experiment or somewhere along the line a result will be obtained which disagrees with observation. It must be admitted that in practice the latter almost universally occurs.

The classical theory of mechanics implies that a pendulum bob once set swinging and let go will oscillate forever, whereas we all know that this is not the case. When such a situation arises—and it has, as a matter of historical fact, arisen in the exploitation of every physical theory that has ever been devised—the scientist can react in either of two ways. He can conclude that the basic postulates of the theory are not plausible, that the theory is all wrong and should be discarded completely. On the other hand, if the number of experimentally confirmed laws deduced from the theory is considerable, he will probably reject this attitude as unduly pessimistic. He will feel that the foundations of the theory are still sound and that the agreement with experiment is not fortuitous but significant. The usual course of action in this case is to attempt to make small changes in the assumptions to see whether the results of the unsatisfactory application cannot be modified in the right direction without leading to incorrect results in the deductions, which originally agreed with experience. A very large part of the development of theoretical physics is devoted to this sort of activity. It may take genius to invent the principal idea or set of ideas behind a given theory, but it still demands much ingenuity and hard work on the part of the less distinguished workers to tidy up the rough spots.

The replacement of one theory by another is not a clear-cut decisive affair that takes place overnight because one fails entirely and another succeeds in meeting all experimental tests. It is a highly complicated process in which many factors enter, among them taste, judgment as to whether the old theory can be patched up to meet the demands of newly acquired experience, and grasp of the possible relations between the theory and theories of related physical phenomena that make it possible to proceed in the direction of greater unity and generality. Actually, the process of theory building and modification has many elements that relate it closely to artistic creativity.

The next step in our discussion requires a closer look at the nature of the postulates at the basis of physical theories. Where do they come from? A theory begins as an act of imagination; it is in essence the creation of a picture in the mind of the scientist. This introduces the problem, but hardly solves it, for how does the scientist get the ideas that form the basic elements of the picture? As we have already suggested, this is a problem in psychology and one to which too little attention has probably been devoted. Too few scientists have ever divulged in any detail the processes they have gone through in setting up their theories, and even when they have discussed the matter, what they have written has not usually been helpful. This may be due partly to a feeling that the line of thought being followed was so straightforward and compelling that it should appear obvious without further comment to all thinking persons. It may also be due to a feeling that inspiration is not discussable. It is true that some very famous scientists have written about flashes of illumination that came to them when, after long periods of unproductive thought, they had attempted to forget the matter at issue in the hope that the subconscious would take over. Such stories are suggestive but do not really instruct. Perhaps there is no instruction to be had in such matters, except by close association with the creative scientist. This is, however, possible for only a few. Psychologists acquainted with science should give this problem greater attention.

One thing appears certain. The thoughts that develop into valuable physical constructs come to those who are equipped to receive them by thorough preliminary preparation in the subject matter being investigated. It is obviously impossible to start to theorize on a scientific subject about which one knows nothing, and it is equally clear that every theorist inevitably is influenced in the creation of new ideas by the ideas he has obtained from others in his previous study.

This suggests two considerations. The first, manifested in the early stages of the development of what we call modern physics (physics from the time of Galileo), is the tendency in the construction of physical theories to use ideas very closely suggested by, and associated with, the phenomena to be described and to be theoretically understood. The second, evident throughout the history of science, is the tendency toward the use of analogy (the explanation of one phenomenon in terms of ideas first introduced to account for another). A good example of the first tendency is presented by Galileo in his discussion of naturally accelerated motion in his *Dialogues Concerning Two New Sciences*: And first of all it seems desirable to find and explain a definition best fitting natural phenomena. For anyone may invent an arbitrary type of motion and discuss its properties; thus, for instance, some have imagined helices and conchoids as described by certain motions which are not met with in nature, and have very commendably established the properties which these curves possess in virtue of their definitions; but we now have decided to consider the phenomena of bodies falling with an acceleration such as actually occurs in nature and to make this definition of accelerated motion exhibit the essential features of observed accelerated motions. And this, at last, after repeated efforts we trust we have succeeded in doing. In this belief we are confirmed mainly by the consideration that experimental results are seen to agree with and exactly correspond with those properties which have been, one after another, demonstrated by us. Finally, in the investigation of naturally accelerated motion we were led, by the hand as it were, in following the habit and custom of nature herself, in all her various other processes, to employ only those means which are most common, simple and easy.[4]

Galileo clearly expresses the conviction that in dealing with any natural phenomenon on a theoretical basis the proper procedure is to utilize constructs directly suggested by the phenomenon itself. He seems to have been convinced that the study of motion would be more successful if he were to confine his postulates to assumptions about observable constructs like velocity and acceleration rather than to introduce vague ideas like impetus in connection with the causes of

---

[4]Galileo, *Dialogues Concerning Two New Sciences* (New York: Macmillan Company, 1914), p. 160.

motion attributed to pushes and pulls and so on. Evidently, Galileo thought he could get something of significance out of the simple postulate that the free vertical fall of a particle near the surface of the earth takes place with constant acceleration. As everyone knows, he succeeded, for this hypothesis leads to the actually observed law of free fall.

Inventors of physical theories from the earliest times to the present have had a fondness for using analogy, sometimes to the disadvantage of a really successful description of experience. By "analogy" we mean here the description of a given phenomenon in terms of ideas that have proved successful in the description of another phenomenon that, as far as all observation goes, is different. Analogy is an illustration of the urge to describe all phenomena with as much economy as possible, with the invention of the minimum number of new ideas. This is a laudable aim and has assisted to a certain extent in the advancement of science. But from another point of view it has hindered progress. By trying to force new experience into the mold of old theory, the scientist has often had to adopt some rather farfetched devices.

The use of analogy in science is closely connected with the employment of pictorial models. An example is the Rutherford atom model, in which the atom is likened to a miniature solar system, the sun being replaced by a massive, positively charged nucleus and the planets by a series of electrons that revolve about the nucleus in orbits that are perturbed ellipses. With this model many properties of atoms corresponding to the various elements of the periodic system can be predicted. It must be confessed that such models usually break down when pressed too far. This certainly occurred in the case of the Rutherford planetary atom model, which needed the introduction of some new and quite unclassical assumptions (those of Niels Bohr) to make it work.

Law. We have defined a physical law as a symbolic shorthand statement descriptive of an observed routine of experience in what might be called the natural domain. As such it is tied to experience, and its scope is definitely limited to the domain it purports to describe. Since it is descriptive, it can only give a partial picture of experience, and there is no element of necessity in its application. In fact, the choice of the word law to symbolize this attempt to describe regularities of experience might be considered a questionable one, since "law" has such an imperative, judicial connotation in everyday language. It is possible that when it came into extensive use during the eighteenth century, there was considerable enthusiasm over an assumed necessary course of nature to which the well-known judicial and theological meanings of the word law might appropriately apply. This enthusiasm has long since evaporated in the face of the growing realization that the actual complexity of our experience severely limits the applicability of every physical law.

The situation takes on a different aspect when we consider the place of law in the context of physical theory. As we have already noted, the fourth stage in the logical schema of a physical theory is the deduction of consequences from the postulates of the theory. We have called these consequences laws, but it is clear that they possess a different logical status from the descriptive laws we have discussed earlier. When, for example, we assume Newton's second law ($F = ma$) to be applicable to the motion of any particle of mass m acted upon by a net resultant force F, and ask ourselves what will be the motion of a particle subject to a constant force, we readily arrive at the consequence that in this motion the displacement must be a quadratic function of the time. This is a logical deduction from the assumption made, and there is no escaping it. If we decide to call this a law relating to motion, it is clear that logically the use of the term is different from that used earlier. The only justification for employing the word law in this case is that we can identify the logical deduction with the descriptive law for certain well-known motions, such as free fall near the earth's surface. But this identification is the key to the whole purpose of a physical theory, which is to portray observed experience in a certain domain. The success of this process is measured by the extent to which the laws deduced from the postulates of the theory can be identified with already established descriptive laws or the ability of the theory to predict new laws that are in turn verified by experiment.

Evaluation. Physical theories are invented in the hope of achieving a better understanding of a portion of our human experience. Every theory has a logical structure that can readily be exposed and through which a firmer grasp of its meaning can be obtained. We must now face the question of what criteria to set up to evaluate how well a given theory achieves its goal. There are several levels on which this can be approached. We can take a positivistic attitude and say simply that a theory is successful to the extent that, on the introduction of appropriate boundary conditions, the laws deduced from it can be identified with experimental evidence. (In other words, the laws agree with experience.) This criterion becomes materially stronger if the theory predicts the existence of regularities in experience that have not hitherto been observed, and if the prediction is verified. This has been taken as a very powerful evidence of the value of a theory, and justly so.

Another criterion by which a theory may be judged is that of truth. This obviously implies a lot more than the positivistic appraisal, for it necessitates a decision as to the meaning of truth, and this is extremely difficult in any scientific context. Presumably, those who believe that a theory should be judged at this level consider it the task of the scientist to discover the whole course of a world of phenomena that exists outside of and independent of the human observer. And having discovered these phenomena, he is to provide a unique explanation for them by means of a theory or set of theories. If and when a theory fits the facts, it will be said to be true, in the sense that the explanation will be final and not subject to upset by further discoveries. It is recognized by most adherents of this view that it is a highly idealistic one, in that no theory has as yet achieved the status of being completely true in this sense. Nevertheless, those who adhere to the criterion of truth believe that certain theories have shown themselves to be so plausible that all they need is further tinkering to make them good for all time. Those who hold this view show more confidence in our present methods of inventing theories than the positivists, and since this confidence may be an important ingredient in the psychological approach of the successful scientist, the view certainly has something to commend it. On the other hand, this same confidence may well be misleading to the layman when he learns of theories that have been discarded because they will not work and have been replaced by others that promise better. This has happened so often in the history of science that it seems more plausible in the logical analysis of scientific theories to discard the use of the notion of truth as it is commonly understood by philosophers and to fall back on the criterion of success, which can at any rate be understood and applied in a definite fashion.

The price that must be paid for the somewhat more positivistic attitude of the criterion of success is a willingness to attribute a purely tentative status to each theory. This inevitably puts stress on the essentially arbitrary character of theories. The positivistic approach appears to have other weaknesses, too. Philosophers have consistently and quite appropriately emphasized that simply because a particular theory leads to deductions agreeing with experience, we have no right to conclude that it necessarily constitutes the best explanation for the given domain of experience. There may well be several other theories that will do as good a job and perhaps even a better one. In fact, the history of science confirms this with many instances of competing theories. On what basis, then, do we decide to give our allegiance to one theory rather than another? There seems to be no simple, clear-cut way in which to distinguish decisively between two scientific theories explaining the same domain of experience. Yet as a practical matter, we have to do it and we do.

What other criteria for the acceptance of a physical theory can we find? An obvious criterion is provided by the principle of parsimony, or the famous "razor" of William of Occam: Entia non sunt multiplicanda praeter necessitatem ("Concepts that yield basic theories must not be multiplied more than is necessary"). Sir Isaac Newton adopted this as the first of his "Rules of Reasoning in Philosophy" at the beginning of his "System of the World" (Book Three of the *Principia*), where he says: "We are to admit no more causes of natural things than such as are both true and sufficient to explain their appearances." He then goes on to amplify this statement: "To this purpose the philosophers say that Nature does nothing in vain, and more is in vain when less will serve; for Nature is pleased with simplicity, and affects not the pomp of superfluous causes."[5]

This has a fine sound, though Newton's confidence in the simplicity of Nature is a judgment probably not shared by the modern scientist. In the light of the present-day creation of experience in the realm of nuclear physics, it is a gratuitous asumption. Nevertheless, most scientists will tacitly agree, other things being equal, that theory which will be most acceptable is the one which operates with the smallest number of independent ideas. Certainly the razor principle has no great trouble in disposing of purely ad hoc theories, in which different postulates have to be invented for each new application of the theory. But the sophistication of modern science has gone far beyond this crude situation. The razor may indeed be of greater applicability

---

[5]I. Newton, *Mathematical Principles of Natural Philosophy* (Berkeley: University of California Press, 1934), p. 398.

to purely mathematical theories, where the constructs are relatively abstract and can be pinpointed, and where they are not identified with ordinary experience.

Much has been made of the concept of simplicity itself as a criterion for evaluating the success of a scientific theory. To some people one particular theoretical point of view appears simpler than another, even though the resulting deductions from the two can be equally well identified with experience. But if one probes deeply into the reason, it usually turns out to be a will-o'-the-wisp and dissolves into inexplicable preference or perhaps more familiarity. We are apt to think of any idea as simple when we have thought long enough about it to become familiar with it. The person who has studied only algebra and geometry in mathematics is apt to think the concepts of calculus mysterious and difficult and far from simple on first encountering them. But if such a person sticks to the subject he can learn it, and then it becomes simple—though higher analysis may then appear in another category again. The effective use of a criterion of simplicity in the evaluation of scientific theories will have to await a much deeper psychological study of the learning process. Meanwhile, scientists will continue to claim that some theoretical viewpoints are simpler than others and hence preferable.

It is sometimes stated scientists explain their preference for one theory over another in terms of the idea of elegance or beauty. Here we get pretty deeply into the realm of aesthetic value judgments, which are, to be sure, only a shade more difficult to deal with than the value judgments inherent in the postulates of a scientific theory. The scientist is forever being confronted with the necessity of expressing preferences, of making choices, and often has a hard time explaining why he made the choice he did. In this he resembles the artist (or humanist in general) who has to face the same kind of situation. It is true that scientists of the eighteenth and nineteenth centuries felt themselves on surer ground with respect to their choices of fundamental attitudes and hypotheses than their successors of the twentieth century. Many of these earlier scientists felt that the assumptions they were making were so naturally connected with, and suggested by, the phenomena to be described and understood that there was really little choice involved. It seemed somehow as if Nature were merely revealing and explaining herself, and man were merely following her lead. The whole development of science in general, however, has cast increasing doubt on this simple interpretation. The twentieth-century scientist can no longer believe that things are what they seem. This makes his job steadily tougher as new experiences accumulate, but it also challenges his imagination and gives him full scope for the development of new and sometimes bizarre ideas, to see how they work.

While the originator of a scientific theory should have full freedom to use his imagination, no matter how esoteric and far removed from everyday experience the constructs and postulates are, it is obviously necessary that somewhere in the development of the theory the constructs or something derived from them be unambiguously identifiable with actual experimental operations. Moreover, this must be possible in more than an ad hoc fashion: the identification should cover the widest possible range of experience. In fact, the more widely the identification can be stretched successfully, the greater the appeal of the theory.

To sum up, the scientist who invents a new theory will use all the weapons in his arsenal to justify its plausibility and to encourage others to test it and try to enlarge the range of its application. Though he may be the first to admit that the workability of a theory in the pragmatic sense is no logical justification for assuming that it provides the final answer, yet he demands the right to continue to exploit a theory if he feels confident that it is an ingenious idea and if it helps him understand a certain domain of experience. In the final analysis, we come back to faith in the value judgments of clever and imaginative people.

Some Philosophical Problems in Science

Science and Philosophy. All aspects of the logical analysis of theorizing involve philosophical questions. Perhaps we ought to justify the assumption that philosophy has any role to play in science at all. Many interpreters deny any serious connection between philosophy and science. They point out, for example, that philosophers seek to understand the world of experience in quite a different way from scientists. For one thing, philosophers rarely seem content to abstract from the totality of experience small domains for intensive study. They wish, rather, to investigate ways of grappling with experience as a whole. They are much exercised over how we can know anything about experience and so have created a whole field of study called epistemology, or the theory of knowledge. When they ask what it means to say that we can know anything, they appear to be going well beyond the scientist's realm of interest, for the scientist takes it for granted that we can know and proceeds confidently from there.

Further, the philosopher raises questions about the nature of those aspects of human experience that the scientist says he wishes to describe and understand. Is this experience something wholly objective in character and independent of human observers, resulting from the existence of a real world, or is it something due entirely to the human observers themselves, something that exists only in their sense impressions? The philosopher thinks that such questions are necessary preliminaries to talking about understanding experience. The scientist on the other hand is apt to become impatient over such lucubrations and will often ask, "What difference does it make?"

This is not an appropriate place to discuss philosophy as a discipline. Interpretations of this differ considerably among professional philosophers themselves. But enough has been said to show that in spite of the scientist's impatience, many of the searching questions of the philosopher do have relevance for physical theorizing. For example, it seems to be wiser for the physicist not to take the general ideas of space and time for granted as something that all intelligent people understand, but to look more closely at how these terms are used and at various possible modifications in their use in physics. Similarly, the philosopher's concern over the relation between events that he expresses in terms of the notion of cause can hardly fail to be considered seriously by the scientist, who is forever dealing with such relations.

Space and Time. Scientific theory is inevitably dependent upon primitive, intuitive notions—the ideas that the scientist takes for granted in order to begin his theory-building activity. The philosopher, however, considers it his duty to examine precisely these fundamental concepts; to him it is obvious that unless the foundations are clearly understood, the superstructure will be shaky indeed. Philosophers have therefore given a great deal of attention to these undefinables. Probably the most important of them all in physics are the notions of space and time.

It is important for scientists to examine and come to terms with the concepts of space and time, which they have commonly left to the scrutiny of professional philosophers. While Newton realized that the concepts of space and time were too important to be altogether overlooked by physicists, in general the language used by Kant and Leibniz to describe these concepts satisfied scientists for a long time. The value of scientific investigation of ideas normally deemed philosophical was finally shown by the work of Einstein and his contemporaries at the beginning of the twentieth century. Their work suggested very strongly that it is not practical to try to separate the concepts of space and time when using them in physics. They are concepts that enter science as inextricably mingled ideas. That the principle of relativity is not a purely academic curiosity but has had a powerful role to play in the development of twentieth-century physics is shown by the fact that atomic and nuclear physics could not have evolved without it. It is scarcely necessary to remind the reader that the famous Einstein mass-energy relation $E = mc^2$ was derived from the theory of relativity and is therefore connected with the attempt by scientists to come to grips with the philosophy of space and time. This should be enough to convince anyone that the philosophical aspects of science are not without practical value.

Operationalism. We have just stated that scientists need to look at the primitive ideas of space and time they employ in the construction of more elaborate concepts used in the development of scientific theories. This leads to a more detailed analysis of how physical constructs come into existence than was offered in connection with the epistemic and constitutive aspects of the definition of physical terms. One side of the problem has attracted much attention from both scientists and philosophers ever since P. W. Bridgman published his first book on the nature of scientific theorizing.[6] Bridgman stressed with great force a point of view about the concepts of physics that has come to be called "operationalism." It is true that he often expressed his dislike for the terms operationalism and operationalist as implying an elaborate philosophical system which he had no interest in setting up. He himself used the term operational analysis, but we shall employ the shorter term as sufficiently indicative of his point of view.

In its most restrictive sense the meaning of operationalism, as Bridgman decribed it, is that physical concepts or constructs shall be defined in terms of actual physical operations. According to this view a concept has no meaning unless it represents an operation that can be

---

[6]P. W. Bridgman, *The Logic of Modern Physics* (New York: Macmillan Company, 1927).

performed in the laboratory and so in this sense is instrumental. Thus it is meaningless to speak of the pressure of a gas, for example, until an operation is described that constitutes the actual measurement of this pressure. The term itself then becomes a symbol to represent an operation or set of operations.

We might say that temperature as a concept in science is defined in terms of the set of operations by which one measures it by a thermometer in the laboratory. Mass is defined by the operation of using a balance, which enables us to assign a number to it. Electric current is defined by the operation of constructing an ammeter, which takes advantage of the heating or magnetic field associated with what we call the flow of current. We could enumerate many physical concepts that can be treated in this way. The point of view of the most thoroughgoing operationalist is that laboratory experiments must be involved in defining any concept used in science. According to him it is definite and unambiguous. It tells us what a concept means in terms of a directive to go and do something specific: hence the appropriateness of the term construct. It is not merely verbal and therefore not susceptible of misunderstanding. It satisfies the best ideals of communication. A student can watch the operational procedure in any particular case and then proceed to carry it out himself. When presented in this context, the idea is a very attractive one, especially in a science that uses a host of concepts, which, if they were to mean different things to different people, could only lead to chaos.

However, another side of the picture becomes apparent once we have taken another look at thoroughgoing operationalism. Take, for instance, the definition of temperature. It is a matter of common observation that there are many kinds of thermometers—among them mercury-in-glass, alcohol-in-glass, constant-volume, and constant-pressure gas thermometers, as well as thermocouples, thermistors, and radiation pyrometers. Which of these shall be used to provide a definition of temperature? Each thermometer involves the use of a highly specific set of laboratory operations. If we were to reply that it really makes no difference, since a measurement by any one of these thermometers under the same conditions will provide the same resulting number, then the rejoinder has to be that this is unfortunately not the case in the world of our actual experience. In the same thermal environment a thermocouple and a liquid-in-glass thermometer—

calibrated in the usual way on the Celsius scale at standard atmospheric pressure, by assigning 0 to the reading when the instrument is placed in melting ice and 100 to the reading in steam, and dividing the interval between these two readings into one hundred equal parts—will not give identical readings in the same environment; the difference usually becomes greater as the temperature of the environment increases. Which thermometer then actually provides the correct temperature? Or must we replace the concept of temperature by a whole set of concepts depending on the particular instrument chosen and the set of operations followed? Even the rigid operationalist realizes that no coherent science can be devised by this procedure. The alternative open to him is to say that we must arbitrarily pick one set of operations to define temperature and then explain why the others do not agree. He is of course at liberty to do this, but unless he can present some reason for his choice that will be plausible to other scientists, his method is again an invitation to confusion and misunderstanding. He is unlikely to make a choice unaccompanied by some reason, but what sort of reason will he give? Already we are out of the realm of rigid operationalism. It seems almost certain that his reason will somehow be tied to physical theorizing, and indeed the choice of the constant-volume gas thermometer as a primary temperature measurement standard is closely connected with the scientific definitions of temperature.

We can make the case against rigid operationalism even stronger by noting that even experimental observations are never quite so definite that all experimenters will agree on how to employ a presumably definite and unambiguous recipe. At any rate, there are many illustrations in the history of science of misunderstandings over experimental processes. The operationalist is likely to reply that this is only adventitious, that as science progresses experimental procedures become more readily described and prescribed.

The strongest case against rigid operationalism rests, however, on considerations not connected directly with experimental operations. If the only concepts allowed into science were those defined in terms of actual laboratory operations, the construction of scientific theories would be impossible. We have already commented on the difficulty encountered in defining temperature in terms of operations in the laboratory. The only reasonable way out of this is to construct a theory of thermal phenomena in which the concept of temperature is defined in terms of its relation to other elements of the theory. Thus in the statistical (molecular) theory temperature is defined in terms of the mean (average) kinetic energy of the molecules. Of course it is necessary to identify this theoretical definition ultimately with temperature as measured by a thermometer. Both theoretical and operational aspects are necessary, as was shown in our discussion of the epistemic (operational) and constitutive (theoretical) aspects of the definition of a construct. Without the constitutive aspects we have no basis for theoretical sciences such as physics. The question thus arises as to how it is possible for any scientist to be a thoroughgoing operationalist in the sense we have attributed to the term. The obvious answer is that it is not possible, unless science is to be reduced to pure empiricism and any attempt to explain phenomena with the help of theories is to be abandoned.

Thoroughgoing or rigid operationalism appears to be outside the mainstream of successful scientific inquiry. The merit of the operational point of view is its emphasis on the importance of the process of identification of the results of scientific theorizing with actual experience. This means that among the concepts of science there must always be some that have both epistemic and constitutive aspects in their definitions. Otherwise, the theories of science would fail to make contact with experience. For this contribution of the operational point of view we should be grateful.

Causality and Determinism. Causality has been the subject of philosophical inquiry for ages, usually in terms of the apposition of cause and effect. That nothing ever takes place without a cause seemed evident to the earliest thinkers. A cause was defined as an occurrence that precedes the given effect, that is always associated with the appearance of the effect, and that is never absent when the effect appears. But many difficulties soon appeared in this simple-minded point of view, among them that in connection with a given phenomenon a number of occurrences often satisfied the conditions set forth, and the question arose as to which condition should be called the real cause. From the very nature of science apparent causal relations among physical phenomena are continually encountered, and so it was inevitable that scientists would have to take some sort of attitude toward this philosophical problem. An illustration of apparent cause and effect in physics is the decrease in the volume of an ideal gas at constant temperature when the pressure is increased. It is tempting to say that the increase in pressure is the cause of the decrease in volume. However, simple reflection shows that it is just as sensible to say that what is really happening when the gas is pressurized is that the volume is decreased—the decrease then becoming the cause of the observed increase in pressure. The notion of cause and effect in this case thus appears to be of little value. Yet the unfailing existence of the relation between pressure and volume does suggest a situation analogous to the philosophical notion of cause and requires the introduction of a principle of causality.

This principle is simply an expression of confidence that physical experience is not a wholly chaotic affair, but that order prevails and can be represented by relations connecting elements of experience—scientific laws. The idea of causality further assumes that the form of such laws is not an explicit function of the time. In other words, if we repeat an experiment on a given gas next week or next year, we expect to find the same result as that obtained today. Moreover, we also expect that the form of the law should be independent of the place where the experiment is performed. "Constants" of nature may change in space and time, but this should not affect the form of scientific laws: the acceleration due to gravity will change from place to place and may even change with the time at a given place, but this should not change the form of the law of falling bodies. The principle of causality in science is simply a reflection of our confidence that there really is regularity in scientific experience and that we are not deluding ourselves when we try to set up scientific laws.

Closely related to the concept of causality is that of determinism, and in the past there has been a tendency to equate the two ideas. Since a given specific cause must of necessity result in a specific effect, the effect is determined; however, as far as science is concerned there is an important difference between causality and determinism.

A scientific theory is said to be deterministic in character if it makes possible the prediction of the future course of a given phenomenon. The simplest illustration of determinism is provided by the theory of classical mechanics. If we know the state of a mechanical system at any one instant, mechanics enables us to predict all past and future states of the system; we may say that the whole temporal behavior of the system is completely determined. The solar system, consisting of the sun and planets and their satellites, constitutes such a system to a good approximation. Knowledge of the state of the system at one instant—of the position and velocity of every body in it—permits the calculation of the position of every body in it for all future times and indeed for all past times also. Hence tables of planetary positions can be prepared with the assurance of precise prediction. The degree of precision is evident in the accuracy with which astronomers can pinpoint the time and exact location of a total solar eclipse, which is caused by the relative positions of the sun and moon as seen from the earth. It is customary to fix in advance the onset of totality within a few seconds of the actually observed time

The success of determinism in celestial mechanics, in the related field of terrestial ballistics, and more recently in missile and artificial satellite technology has made a powerful impression on all who use mechanical concepts and can understand how they work. Certainly the thinkers of the eighteenth and nineteenth centuries, impressed by the success of Newton and his followers, tended increasingly to identify determinism with causality, thus introducing a certain amount of confusion into the methodology of modern science.

The History of Science

The History of Science and Its Problems. A scientist's attitude toward the history of science is obviously based on his conception of history in general. Various epitomizing definitions of this branch of knowledge have been offered.[7] A satisfactory one is that of William Henry Walsh, according to whom history is "an intelligent reconstruction of the past."[8] His definition emphasizes the two important characteristics of history: the accurate presentation of the record of the past wherever found and the rational interpretation of what took place. While Walsh's definition does not specify the precise meaning of "the past," most professional historians prefer to construe it as meaning the past of the human race. To the scientist, however, it means the past of nature and our universe as a whole.

A difficulty arises from Walsh's point of view at the very outset. Science as we know it today is a well-established discipline, involving specific types of mental attitudes toward experience and its creation.

---

[7]R. B. Lindsay, *The Role of Science in Civilization* (New York: Harper & Row, 1963), chapter 5.

[8]W. H. Walsh, *Philosophy of History, An Introduction* (New York: Harper Torchbooks, 1960), p. 29.

What elements in the past, especially the remote past, should be recognized as corresponding to the science of our time? This must be an arbitrary decision. Where the Greeks make statements about the motion of bodies the difficulty is not apparent, and we accept their statements as descriptions of a branch of ancient physics. But when the discourse is about dreams and demons, or about temperament as related to the "heat" of the human body, the relationship to modern scientific concepts is not so clear. Perhaps the ancient thinkers used such concepts to help them understand that part of experience now called science, but it is impossible to be certain in all cases.

This leads to another difficulty. Granted a written record that says something about experience, exactly what do the words in the record mean? This is not just a problem of adequate translation from an ancient language to our own. We shall assume that a reliable linguist has done this job satisfactorily. Almost inevitably, however, he will not be a scientist and will be forced to give the words their common meaning. But even in modern science, common terms are given meanings entirely different from those they have in ordinary speech, and this was certainly also the case in antiquity.

The scholar-scientist can of course examine the material carefully for internal clues about the meaning of words and other expressions. In the final analysis, however, he must make some further arbitrary judgments. In essence, what he does is to frame a theory about the nature of the historical material he is trying to understand. Theory in history is similar to theory in science. The fundamental constructs of science correspond to the terminology of the historical record, and the postulates to hypotheses as to the meaning assigned to historical terminology. The conclusions form an estimate of the success of earlier scientists' methods of coping with experience. The historian of science endeavors to reconcile the thoughts and methods of the past with the modern way of understanding the experience in question; otherwise, the whole study would be meaningless. This is perhaps the principal assumption of all history—that it is possible to reconstruct the past in terms that make it intelligible to the present. It is scarcely sufficient, for example, to find and reproduce Babylonian astronomical tables, so that a modern reader can see merely what they look like. The task of the historian of astronomy is not achieved until he has explained just how these tables were used and the theory by which they were constructed.

The task of the historian of science is clearly a very difficult one. In addition to being a competent scientist, he must also be enough of a historian to be able to deal successfully with the problems of reconstructing the past. Such a combination of talents is rare, and the preparation of scholars specifically in this field is a relatively recent development. In spite of the existence of the classical work of Pierre Duhem on the history of mechanics and the work of Alexandre Koyre on Galileo, it cannot be said that the history of science has made great advances. The number of professional historians of science has grown very slowly, and the fields covered are limited. Even in the development of science in the seventeenth and eighteenth centuries, for example, there is much that is obscure, though the publication of the collected writings of the distinguished scientists of that time has been actively fostered.

There are indications of an increasing contemporary interest in the history of science. One sign is a growing concern to make the record complete and accessible. Not too much can be done about this for earlier periods, but something can be accomplished for contemporary science or at any rate the science of the past seventy-five to one hundred years. It is obvious that if there is no record there can be no history. Not all scientists are historically minded and so do not always appreciate the importance of retaining notes, records of experimental measurements, precise descriptions of equipment, and correspondence with colleagues. The successors and heirs of scientists are apt to be even more careless and casual about such matters, so that much material of the greatest value to the historian of science is destroyed or scattered and effectively lost. To prevent this in the case of physics in the United States, the American Institute of Physics, assisted by a grant from the National Science Foundation, has been carrying on a project to gather material useful for the history of American physics in the twentieth century. In addition to locating and encouraging the preservation of manuscript material left by distinguished American physicists now deceased, the project endeavors to build up a body of source material contributed by living physicists and to gather information about the location of the equipment they used in their experiments. The records of research published in the professional scientific journals do not tell the full story of the mental processes followed by the investigator; for this his notes are often more useful. Attempts are also being made to interview older physicists and to make tape recordings of their views as to the significance of their work. When used with due caution, this kind of record can be of great historical value in answering questions of priority of discovery and other important questions. At any rate the project should provide a more detailed and accurate record of twentieth-century American physics than can be expected to result from the usual chance accumulation of information.

It must be admitted that there are competent scientists who gravely doubt the value of such concern with the history of their discipline. Some frankly take the stand that no matter how hard the historian of science tries to unearth the truth about a particular discovery, it will elude him. These scientists therefore conclude that the whole activity leads only to frustration and to misconceptions of the development of the science. Of course, precisely the same sort of attack can be made on history as a whole.

Even when the practicing scientist does not quarrel with the cultural value of the history of science for the general public, he is often convinced that it has no practical value for the scientist in his research. This view has been expressed with some force by James B. Conant, who is willing to admit that an acquaintance with the science of the past fifty to seventy-five years may be desirable, but cannot see any use in going back any further.[9] However, a reasonable interpretation of many lines of development in the history of physics effectively refutes this view.[10] Regardless of the difficulties associated with the history of science, it is clear that they will be overcome and that the subject will ultimately assume its proper place in the intelligent reconstruction of the past that is the task of history in general.

In the light of our earlier discussion of the relation between science and philosophy, what, if any, is the connection between the history and philosophy of science? It is plausible to hold the view that these two disciplines have no essential connection with each other. One might hold that the history of science is merely the record of what took place and of who did what and when. This would reduce history essentially to an anecdotal status, and its interest to scientists would be minimal. But the record in the case of the history of science is supremely important, just as it is for any branch of history. The record alone,

---

[9]J. B. Conant, "History in the Education of Scientists," *American Scientist* 48 (1960): 528.

[10]Lindsay, *The Role*, p. 120.

however, is not history: it must be interpreted and related to our present knowledge. Since interpretation inevitably involves philosophical matters of the kind already discussed, the history of science, to be of any value, must be inextricably related to its philosophy.

The evolution of the concept of energy—one of the great developments in the history of science—is an example of this inextricable relationship. The germ of the concept may well have arisen in the idea of invariance, the notion that something stays constant in the midst of change. On the other hand, it is possible, and has seemed more plausible to some authorities, to seek the germ of the idea of energy in the presumptive impossibility of perpetual motion. This view was favored by Ernest Mach. It is for the philosophy of science to decide to what extent these two views can be reconciled, or if they cannot be reconciled, which of the two gives the more basic and compelling view of the modern concept of energy. Examples of this kind of philosophical problem occur in all aspects of the history of science.

A related question is whether, if we cannot effectively study the history of science without reckoning with philosophical problems, we can hope to study philosophical questions relating to present-day science without some acquaintance with the historical evolution of the ideas in question. This is a controversial matter. It can be argued that philosophical problems, such as those connected with modern quantum mechanics, can be profitably discussed without reference to the history of the subject. For example, the meaning of measurement in quantum mechanics is a part of the philosophy of science, but it can be handled merely as an exercise in logical analysis, depending on the various forms of the theory. It seems, however, that a more meaningful procedure would be to examine the meaning of measurement as the idea has developed historically. From this standpoint, a philosophical problem in modern science profits from a knowledge of history. For all practical purposes the philosophy and history of science are really inextricably related.

No one is in a position to make a valid projection over a wide span of time of the future of science with any greater likelihood of success than the predictors of the course of human history in general. We can be sure, however, that as long as human curiosity and imaginative power endure, science will always make a significant contribution to the creation, description, and understanding of nature. Science will continue to provide a framework on which we construct our civilization, and in this sense it will always be an important cornerstone in the liberal arts tradition. That an understanding of science is vital in a liberal arts environment comes with the realization that the physical world is domain for all human experience, and nature places virtually absolute conditions on how we may operate within this domain. Each individual is but a minute segment of the cosmos, but that small fragment of nature obviously is of genuine importance to every person since it includes their own selves.

Science is not adequate, in and of itself, as a total philosophy. We must have the other liberal arts disciplines: philosophy, history, literature, music, and so forth. Suppose we were asked to choose between retaining science in the liberal arts tradition, or maintaining the humanistic liberal arts program but excluding science from our universities, libraries, and other intellectual pursuits. Without science to provide a fundamental knowledge of natural philosophy we would soon become the victims of ignorance and superstition. Fear of the unknown and unpredictable would arise from every unexplained natural phenomenon. Mankind would soon be returned to a state of dependence on the witch doctor, the charlatan, and the religious "prophet."

Now consider the other possibility. Suppose we transform all our colleges and universities entirely into technical institutes and scientific research centers, destroy the literary classics, forbid the practice and teaching of religion, and permit no philosophy to be taught, no pictures to be painted, no music to be played, and no poetry or novels to be authored or even read. Obviously, this situation is unthinkable, for without the full range and scope of the liberal arts we would sacrifice the ability to control and restrain the unfettered power of science for harming society as well as helping it.

In this essay, science has been considered as an important facet of a liberal arts education—as a method for describing, creating, and understanding human experience. In addition to the description and creation of experience the method of science includes understanding— the attempt to discover why experience manifests the particular order or pattern exemplified by scientific laws. Understanding results from the construction of theories that are imaginative visions of the mind, pictures of the world as it might be, and which, if it were, would produce observed experience. The fact that science is the creation of people has been emphasized throughout this discussion. Science has a philosophy and a history, and these factors play a most significant role in explaining what science is all about and why it is an essential element in the traditional liberal arts education.

American Leadership and the Failure of the Humanities

Kurt Corriher

Cynical spirits have been predicting the downfall of the United
States since before its birth—and probably of all other societies since
the human species first banded together and formed customs which
were subject to change. As a consequence educated Americans habitu-
ally ignore the doomsayers, assuming that the underlying strength of
our democratic institutions will carry us through. Yet there is no
denying that the past fifteen years have been a particularly discourag-
ing era in the history of the nation, and despite the resurgence of hope
brought on by a fresh administration, there remains a stubborn sense
of unease in the American psyche. Both public opinion polls and
behavior on Wall Street indicate that this year the traditional honey-
moon optimism is tempered by unusual caution. The prevailing attitude is tenaciously wait-and-see.

To be sure, our economy is still floundering toward an uncertain future; violent crime and assorted other social ills are on the increase; and there is no longer any question that our military defenses have deteriorated significantly. But these are all combatable problems, and despite them, the nation remains fundamentally secure and prosperous. The uneasiness which is dampening a normally buoyant cycle in the national spirit must have a broader source. In fact the problem is not so much despair at specific ills as it is a loss of confidence in the ability of America's leaders to cope with our difficulties.

From the Viet Nam debacle, through Watergate and the bungled Olympic boycott, to the Iranian Revolution, America's authorities have demonstrated a penchant for misjudgment which has dismayed not only the American populace but most other nations as well. With an apparently unerring instinct for the wrong policy, recent leaders have steered us into a period of economic and social decline which has been steeper and more threatening than anyone imagined possible even a decade ago. It is difficult to specify who is at fault. Presidents blame Congress. Congress blames the bureaucracy. Liberals blame conservatives. Conservatives blame liberals. And they all get together once a month or so and blame the Arabs.

Yet the external difficulties we face today are child's play compared with those of previous episodes in the nation's history. Through a civil war, two world wars, and a cataclysmic depression, the American people managed to come together and conquer every challenge to their safety and prosperity. Even today the Japanese (far more dependent on imported energy than the U.S.) have so far managed to cope quite well and are humming along in unparalleled prosperity. We have never been free of problems from abroad. The difference today is that we seem incapable of dealing with them in a unified, effective manner. If nations with fewer resources can, and we cannot, than a reasonable conclusion is that something has gone wrong with our leadership. Indeed something has gone wrong, and in the absence of competent leadership the nation has splintered into squabbling factions, so-called "special interest groups" who are striving at cross-purposes and often pursuing narrow, short-sighted goals.

America could probably shrug off one or two incompetent presidents and recover, but distressingly, our current leadership crisis appears to be more deeply rooted. It cripples us at many levels. True statesmen are a vanishing species, and in their place stand image-conscious politicians, approving or rejecting legislation on the basis of current popularity. (Government-by-public-opinion-poll is the natural result of a leadership vacuum.) Our finest executives have guided the American steel and automobile industries to the brink of ruin, while the nation's institutions of higher learning have rushed to render themselves incapable of fulfilling their function—and therein lies the heart of the problem. For a failure of leadership is, inevitably, a failure of education, and if education has failed, then our colleges and universities, the cornerstone of the system, are ultimately at fault. It is true that many of today's students are emerging from secondary school barely able to read and write, but it was the universities who trained their teachers, and it was the universities who produced the politicians responsible for larger social disruptions which have adversely affected primary and secondary education. Of course it is people who fail, not institutions, and so the weakness of American leadership can at last be traced to those who are responsible for American higher education—our illustrious and erudite college faculties, the learned, the intellectual elite.

In fact we can focus still more specifically on the faculty of the traditional humanities disciplines: philosophy, theology, history, language, and the various arts. These are the disciplines which form the core of almost every college education, and they are the parents of the still—infant social sciences whose "new class" professionals were so roundly rejected in the last election. The natural sciences, generally speaking, have delivered the research capability and high technology which society demanded of them. We in the humanities, on the other hand, have not even been able to decide what our goals are, much less achieve them. We get impatient and irritated when students ask, "What does it have to do with the *real* world?" We get irritated because we do not know, and impatient because we do not care. The usual dodge is to mutter a few vague phrases like "end in itself" or "self-enrichment," and then pacify them with the smug assurance that they will understand in later years. I submit that the primary goal of undergraduate education in the humanities—even the core courses designed for science majors—can be formulated in a succinct phrase: to create individuals of excellence for the leadership of our society. At present it clearly is failing in that mission.

The need for such individuals of excellence is undeniable. A tragic misconception of the age is that leadership is a matter of efficient management, best handled by skilled technicians. As a result, those capable of building an efficiently functioning organization have been rewarded with promotion and authority. The ability to set goals for that organization or to judge the long-range consequences of its functions are skills rarely considered. When Jerry terHorst resigned as Gerald Ford's press secretary, he reportedly complained of Ford's lack of "vision," and it was often said of Jimmy Carter that under his presidency the nation was "overmanaged" and "underled." Unfortunately these presidents merely reflected trends which are evident at other levels of leadership as well. Every day hundreds of thousands of civil servants fill millions of forms which keep the bureaucracy functioning, but with no one adequately supervising what it does or does not accomplish, just as automobile executives labor to perfect techniques for the efficient production of cars nobody wants. In other words, we are burdened with a concept of leadership which stresses efficiency in day-to-day operations, but neglects the formulation of sound overall objectives. Such objectives should be the first priority of leadership, and the ability to fashion them is precisely the skill which training in the humanities should develop.

The cadre of technician-managers who form the American leadership caste exhibit one particularly egregious deficiency: a lack of perspective—both in time (historical) and in space (cultural). They are masters of the parts, but blind to the exigencies of the whole. In the 1980 election candidates sought to drown each other in an ocean of statistics. Debate on all major issues, from busing to defense, found candidates squaring off armed with a pocket calculator and a sheaf of computer printouts. Like no other campaign in history, this was a war of numbers. Of course there is nothing wrong with a firm grasp of the nuts and bolts of any issue—unless, as has recently been the case, nobody seems to realize that they should all fit together. Candidates approach government as a grab bag of discrete and unconnected issues, each with its specific problems, numbers, and "solutions"—in short, as an aggregate of management tasks. That there could be a link between, say, the productivity rate and attitudes toward abortion, or between opposition to the draft and the high cost of medicare, seems never to occur to anyone. There is virtually no discussion (and one must assume very little thought) expended on the question of just what constitutes a healthy and prosperous society. What are the nation's fundamental needs? Our politicians apparently feel that those needs are accelerated depreciation allowances and peripatetic missiles in the Utah desert.

Certainly immediate issues are important, and a grasp of mundane realities is crucial for effective action. But to determine where we are going, it is necessary to understand who we are and where we have been. It would be comforting to feel that our leaders, in some corner of their psyches, were aware that our generation is but a blink in history, that our present reality has been shaped in part by decisions made centuries ago, and that decisions taken today will exercise profound influence on human society when our gravestones have crumbled— assuming of course that there still is a human society. Few congress-men, for example, seem clearly aware that cultures evolve, grow, mature, and die—much less seem to be concerned about where our nation might now stand in any such historical phase, or how individu-als can influence the process. Many a politician can discuss isolated national problems, but virtually no one shows an awareness of the drift of Western Civilization as a whole.

Provincialism has been endemic to the American population since the first child was born on the vast and isolated soil of this continent. Our ignorance of and insensitivity toward other cultures is legendary. Oddly, it has grown worse rather than better in this era of advanced means for travel and communication. Our notorious incompetence in foreign languages has reached new heights precisely when the ability to communicate on an international level is more crucial than ever. Indifference, even hostility toward foreign languages is merely one symptom of a far more dangerous disease: contempt for cultures we do not understand. Among the uneducated, provincialism is expected, but when such ignorance extends to congressmen, senators, and presi-dents, then our ability to function in the international community is dangerously impaired. The vast majority of our diplomatic personnel and their dependents living abroad (usually in closed-off American compounds) cannot even read a local newspaper, much less converse with the citizens of the country where they are posted. Small wonder that we have been guilty of such colossal misjudgments in Southeast Asia and the Middle East. Even today we throw up our hands and declare the behavior of foreign peoples "lunatic" or "irrational" simply because we cannot fathom motivations beyond those common to the American view of life.

Now that we no longer have a world monopoly in technology, American ineptitude in international commerce is becoming a standing joke—a joke which costs our economy billions of dollars a year. In the past two decades our share of the world market has plunged from twenty to twelve per cent. The director of a West German trade institute recently complained to me in exasperation that American clothing exporters simply cannot comprehend that Europeans dress differently from Americans—let alone that French, German, Italians, Swiss, and others all prefer their own unique styles.

Blind foreign policies and losses in international trade are merely the two most obvious examples of the consequences of cultural ignorance. The gravest weakness is far more subtle. It has been said that whoever knows nothing of a foreign language knows nothing of his own. The same is true of culture. Like no other developed nation, America lacks perspective on itself. How can leadership be innovative when it cannot even perceive the difference between human nature and a merely cultural trait? How can it guide a society through treacherous times with no awareness of the fundamental ideals and assumptions on which that society is based? There are other value systems, different ways of perceiving human life, which have flourished for centuries on other portions of this globe, yet to most of America's leaders, they might never have existed. It is no accident that our elected officials blunder helplessly back and forth among a handful of worn-out policies, none of which is currently adequate. Never having sincerely confronted alternative views of life, they have a stunted sense of what is possible. Variety is the fuel of imagination, and thus of creativity, and without creativity there can be only management—no leadership.

It is relatively easy to show that the study of history and foreign civilizations helps develop historical and cultural perspective. But what of philosophy, literature, and the other arts? Are these the frivolous subjects which most Americans perceive them to be? (Fewer than twenty percent of all undergraduate degrees are currently being awarded in any humanities discipline.) Far from it. To begin with, art is also history. Art, in whatever form, is an expression of the history of the human spirit, and as such it is at least as crucial to an understanding of our past (and present) as is the history of wars, treaties, and the like. Moreover, art portrays an aspect of human existence sadly neglected in American life, and by America's leadership—the irrational impulse in man.

The power of that impulse, for both good and evil, has long been underestimated in our practical society, but it has never been so dangerously ignored by our leaders as in recent decades. We define every problem in terms of economics, and doggedly toss money into the South Bronx where it only feeds the fires of a burned-out urban wasteland. When it is obvious that wealth and high technology have not brought the citizenry any greater happiness than they possessed in poorer times—perhaps less, considering the soaring suicide rate among the young—why do our leaders continue to view every problem as a question of budget? Why can they not realize (as did Churchill, for example) that there is such a thing as a national will, and that individuals can and must exercise profound influence over it? Why are they so inept at rallying the nation to unity and sacrifice? Why do they dismiss issues of the human spirit with a few obligatory platitudes? Why do they seem unaware that to be human is to be fragile and temporary, and that "projected ratios" and "earnings equivalents" are merely the servants of love, and loneliness, and fear?

The answer clearly lies in the failure of humanities education in America. History, theology, literature—the study of these subjects does not directly teach an individual how to run a service station, let alone the State Department, nor should it. What it should do, *when properly directed*, is develop the full mental and spiritual resources of the individual. It should instill respect for excellence. It should teach a man or woman to look not only at the obvious but at the subtle—and no less essential. It should liberate creative powers. It should train the mind to think in depth as well as breadth. It should instill an awareness of the complexity of life and help develop the character and confidence to face that complexity. The humanities should provide an understanding of human history from which to create cogent responses to today's circumstances.

Effective education in the humanities could give us corporate leaders capable of supplying goods and services which contribute to mankind's well-being, rather than merely distract from his emptiness. It could give us political leaders as sensitive to the needs of the nation's spirit as to the gross national product. In short, it could produce not mere competence, but stature as well—individuals prepared to meet the demands of true leadership. The obvious question is, since virtually every college student undergoes at least some humanities training, why is American leadership so deficient in the qualities that such training should provide? That brings us to the sad state of the humanities in higher education today.

In the public mind the model of someone well educated in the humanities is a college English professor—or at least the stereotype of one. We all know good old Professor X with his rumpled suit and scuffed shoes, shuffling to the library, arms clutching a bundle of books, and mind permanently exiled among the contemplative mysteries of Alexander Pope. He knows everything about Milton and nothing about his checking account. He writes books on aesthetic theory but dissolves into tears if his fan belt breaks on the freeway. He is master of the abstract and theoretical but utterly lacking in common sense, barely able to cope with the practical world. He is harmless enough, generally speaking, but God forbid the fellow should ever be allowed to make an important decision. Related to this stereotype is the prevailing attitude that the humanities have no practical value whatsoever. Literature, music, philosophy, and the like are all right for those (such as professors) who have nothing better to do, but whoever wants to succeed in the society at large had better avoid such studies whenever possible.

There are a number of reasons why middle-class America holds this view. We have a history of virulent anti-intellectualism from the Puritan denunciation of universities as "Stews of Anti-Christ" to Spiro Agnew's clever coinage of "effete intellectual snobs." Such attitudes survive, however, only because our college faculties, the nation's intellectual elite, have allowed them to do so. In fact we not only allow it, we actually contribute to the notion that humanities study is mere self-indulgence and can even spoil one's potential for practical success.

There is so much wrong with humanities education in America today that it is difficult even to begin a discussion of the ills. The roots of the problem stretch back to the rise of European liberalism and the eventual establishment of mass democracies—a political reality with which intellectuals have never come to terms. We have instead retreated into an invisible exile where, cut off from our natural responsibilities within society, we have grown increasingly decadent and petty. Of course the popular view of Professor X is distorted and unfair. It is also, like many stereotypes, an exaggeration of traits which are essentially accurate. College faculties are remarkably inept at dealing with practical matters, and an objective observer could hardly blame the businessman who declared he would not hire a college professor to run a peanut stand.

What else might one expect from a group of people who maintain an elaborate ivory tower, originally constructed to safeguard academic liberty, but now functioning only to protect faculty members from what we ourselves refer to—only half jokingly—as the "real world." The ivory tower no longer prevents outside influences from controlling the educational process—through Madison Avenue tactics in recruiting students, the rise of a middle-management caste which dominates decision-making, and so forth—but professors still cling to that portion of the old tower which serves as a personal barrier against the common machinery of society. College campuses, with their spacious quadrangles, manicured walkways, and ivy-covered halls are havens of refuge, as insulated as possible from the vulgar hustle of commercial civilization. Certainly there is no harm in maintaining an atmosphere conducive to study, but the halls of academe long ago transcended that modest goal and began to assume the isolating characteristics of a monastery.

Here again one must be careful to distinguish between the humanities and other academic fields. Passage in and out of the tower is relatively fluid for those in the natural sciences, business, or law. Summer work, even lengthy leaves of absence for private consulting or industrial or medical research are common and accepted in such fields—even encouraged. Among humanities faculties, however, there is an unspoken taboo against any sort of liaison with the vulgar world outside. Free time should be spent in the library pursuing the holy grail of scholarship—not out in the market place, dirtying oneself among the rabble. (One literature professor I know was the target of contemptuous gossip because he ran a lucrative automobile repair shop in his spare time.) We justify the maintenance of our monastery by fostering the illusion that teaching is somehow a sanctified pursuit. We even employ the vocabulary of religion, speaking in hushed tones of our "sacred" duties, or of the "devotion" of the true scholar. Faced with disgracefully inadequate salaries, we comfort ourselves with a weary sigh and some soothing self-praise about the sacrifices we make for our noble cause (whatever it is). Dabbling with political power is even more suspect than a commercial enterprise, and the occasional humanities professor who runs for public office must brave the scorn of his colleagues. Politics is not for the pure. In short we have insulated ourselves within what we call the "academic community," infused it with a semi-religious aura, and settled into complacent little academic routines, thereby supplying the "real world" with ample material for its stereotype. It is hardly surprising that the humanities have become unattractive for our more ambitious students who seek activity and involvement.

Just because we shy away from the mundane machinery of a working society does not, however, prevent us from passing judgment upon others. In fact we have adopted the safest possible attitude toward society at large—that of passive opposition. Irving Kristol, taking a cue from Lionel Trilling, calls it "the adversary culture." We hold ourselves above the necessities of commercial life, but not above criticism of it. In one of our sillier delusions we are fond of assuring each other that society needs us to "teach it the difference between right and wrong." In truth, with the exception of an occasional lunatic, the world has a pretty good idea of right and wrong. (In any event I doubt that academics exemplify extraordinary moral rectitude.) What society needs are leaders who can maximize the right and minimize the wrong in the daily course of human life. We do not need more people to expatiate upon ethical theory in our lecture halls. We need people who can handle the far more difficult and complex task of furthering justice on our streets. Academics are great at bringing society's flaws to the attention of the young, but we fail to develop them into leaders who might guide society away from those flaws. Certainly it is not our business to propagandize "solutions" for specific issues, but it *is* our business to see that the young develop the character, confidence, and understanding with which to act effectively when they assume responsibility. We should provide the palette and brush. It will be up to them to paint the picture.

Unfortunately most professors do not consider the practical realities of leadership to be even indirectly their concern. We deplore the insensitivity of our leaders towards the inner needs of man. We lament that they possess no deeper understanding of historical and cultural complexity. We bemoan the shallowness and ineffectiveness of their policies. But we fail to see our own students as leaders of the future who, if properly trained, might overcome those deficiencies. We do not even encourage them to aspire to positions of authority. In fact we achieve precisely the opposite. We pass on to them our disdain for practical activism, our contempt for the vulgarity of commerce and politics. We teach them that the humanities are for personal enrichment, not practical application. We hold up an ideal of the quiet, contemplative life of scholars (such as ourselves) who spurn the scurry and bustle of life in the streets. Small wonder that the humanities seem so irrelevant to the bulk of society. We have made them so. Our scorn for practical affairs is communicated to our students in a thousand subtle ways. We are receptive to Antigone's grand passion—less so to the sober demands of leadership facing Creon. We treat our topics as if they existed in a vacuum, remote from events in the evening newspaper. The humanities, we constantly imply, have nothing to do with the dynamic activism required for leadership. We are failing to produce competent leaders because we make no attempt to do so. Having isolated *ourselves* from the realities of a functioning society, we draw our students with us for four crucial years of their transition to adulthood.

As freshmen enter the classroom building where I teach, they encounter the bust of a former professor with an inscription identifying him as a "profound and versatile scholar, effective and beloved teacher, friendliest and gentlest of men." No doubt he was all of those, and I have no wish to belittle virtues such as friendliness and gentleness. I maintain, however, that they receive a distorted and unrealistic emphasis in the ideal which we present to our students. Once again we betray a penchant for passive values. *Don't* be cruel. *Don't* be brutal. *The Wall Street Journal* reported that a study of 200 recently hired college graduates indicated that they have far less interest in leadership than did their predecessors of twenty-five years ago. Researchers discovered that today's graduates "don't want to take charge in group situations." How could they after four years of an educational atmosphere so hostile towards take-charge personalities? The emphasis is on the benign, the tolerant, the passive—all admirable virtues at appropriate moments, but at times the well-being, perhaps even the survival, of a society requires actions that are neither friendly nor gentle.

We celebrate an all-encompassing intellectual doubt, but rarely mention that action necessitates, at some point, the adoption of principle. In fact the very concept of necessity, especially harsh necessity, is slighted in the humanities education we offer—buried beneath our zeal for the refined and beautiful. Yet all the great writers we claim to teach have recognized and wrestled with this critical fact of life. (Matthew Arnold wrote of "the high / Uno'erleaped Mountains of Necessity.") Recognizing that reality dishes out cruelties, compulsions, and inevitabilities is a crucial step in the maturation of a leader and should, therefore, be a crucial element of his education. Our failure to make it such is hardly surprising, considering the elaborate pains we take to avoid necessity ourselves. What is the ivory tower today but a fortress for the faculty against the common necessities of our culture?

We influence character development by our own example as well, and there too we only discourage leadership potential. Boldness, determination, decisiveness—such qualities rarely rear their ugly heads in academe. In fact they are felt to be in bad taste. Whenever possible we choose to do nothing at all, as the safest course of action— or, rather, inaction. I recall one academic department which was terrorized for years by an ill-tempered and incompetent secretary. No one had the courage to fire her. Faculties jealously insist on their prerogative to forge educational policy, yet no individual professor accepts responsibility for what does, or more often does not happen in such things as curriculum planning. I once sat on a faculty committee charged with developing a proposal for revising the school's general education requirements. The committee was finally dissolved by an impatient dean because we were unable to reach a decision after two years of regular meetings. Walter Kaufmann calls it "decidophobia" and it is epidemic on college campuses. Faculties routinely spend years bickering over issues that could be dispatched in a week. Why? Because we reject authority (and leadership) with all its vulgar implications and insist instead on our right to mull about as an ineffectual herd, thereby preserving our stereotype while providing abominable examples for the future leaders of society.

In the past decade college faculties have uncharacteristically sprung into action—unfortunately in a way consistent with our fondness for negativism. The difficult task of creating and establishing effective educational policies still eludes us, but we have learned to *abolish* with a fervor the Huns would have envied. In fact, though it has hardly been noticed by the general public, American institutions of higher learning have all but abolished education in the humanities. It began in the late sixties when students began to grumble that not everything was perfect with our required core curricula. Most of us could agree to that. We could not agree on a positive alternative though, so we just dismantled curriculum requirements and left it at that. There are still plenty of humanities *courses* around, but very little humanities education. Our eighteen-year-old freshmen are blissfully unaware that one course has anything to do with another, or that all aspects of human knowledge are complexly interrelated, and we have agreed that if they do not want to know, then it is not our business to tell them. Oddly we still feel that it is a professor's obligation to select and organize the materials for a given course, but to provide similar guidance on a broader scale now seems somehow presumptuous, if not downright undemocratic.

That brings up the idea of necessity again. Having avoided it so long themselves, America's college faculties are growing increasingly reluctant to inflict it upon their students. Goethe long ago recognized that the best way to teach someone is to treat him as if he already were what you wish him to become. I am not sure what, if anything, we wish our students to become, but it is clearly *not* responsible adults, capable of meeting demands and willing to conquer difficulty. As we were dealing with the protests against course requirements we also were told that tests and grades put students under unpleasant pressure (nasty necessity again), and that our evaluation procedures encouraged shallow attitudes toward learning. Given the fact that society, and even the students themselves, unquestionably need evaluations of achievement and potential, it would have been reasonable to meet these (partly legitimate) complaints with a reform of our system for obtaining those evaluations. Typically, we chose to abolish them instead. Grade inflation was sufficient in most cases, but where that was not enough, we came up with the now popular pass-fail system, whereby we impress upon our students that in personal achievement the standards are "good enough" and (rarely) "not good enough." With that the idea of excellence was banished from the nation's campuses, soon to be accompanied into exile by term papers, essay exams, required class attendance, and everything else that stood in the way of painless education. Certainly many of the demands placed on students in the past were counterproductive and in need of change. Unfortunately, faculties proved themselves incapable of carrying out reforms, and instead simply yielded to the pressures of the moment and *called it* reform.

The plunge in academic standards needs no elaboration. It is finally obvious to all, though each of us blames someone else. The important point is that we have done a grave disservice to our students and, more importantly, to our nation. It is challenge which promotes achievement, and achievement which fuels interest—not the other way around. Young men and women rise to the expectations of their mentors, rarely above them. By denying them challenge we deny them both skills and self-assurance. When we pull them into our private academic sanctuary, we abort the natural process of maturation and then send them back into the world with a deficient education, an increasingly meaningless diploma, and the cruel illusion that they are prepared to meet the demands of adult reality. Life, we are teaching them, is supposed to be easy. As a consequence more and more of our students are finding that their real education begins at graduation. Worst of all we place our entire culture in jeopardy by failing to graduate bold, self-assured young men and women, willing to engage adversity and capable of conquering it. In short, no one is training tomorrow's leaders.

Although the humanities faculty sets the tone for most of America's colleges and universities, the deterioration in higher education is not entirely our fault. We have faced enormous pressures beyond our control. In the fifties and sixties, as a college education ceased to be regarded as training for society's elite and became instead a sort of continuation of public high school, the stampede of students compelled wholesale compromises. The runaway egalitarianism of the seventies put further pressure on educational standards, and today a severe financial and demographic crunch is posing the most dangerous threat ever to higher education in America. The slashing of faculty positions and the death of whole institutions has triggered a scramble for warm bodies to put in our classrooms, resulting in a massive assault on what little is left of academic standards.

We could not have prevented these broad social and cultural changes even if it had been desirable to do so. What we could have done is adjust to a changing situation without sacrificing our mission. Instead we remained bogged down in our accustomed passivity and simply capitulated to the onslaught of circumstances. We allowed events to take control of our institutions while we formed committees and sat around worrying about what was happening rather than taking effective action to counter it. The consequences of our failure are monumental. The fate of the entire society is dependent on the educational process, and American higher education, particularly in the humanities, has deteriorated into a state of virtual impotence. Still the humanities faculties mull around in confusion and indecision, trying to deny what most of us know in our hearts—that the humanities are in desperate trouble. We need thorough, fundamental, by our standards even radical reform, and we need it immediately.

Whatever changes we may eventually undertake, the starting point must be a hard, fresh look at our purpose, our *raison d'etre*. Public support is failing, and it is failing because the public no longer believes in our value. Instead of whining about the hopeless philistinism of the masses, we should ask ourselves if we really *are* as useful to humanity as the plumber who earns twice our salary. At present there is legitimate doubt. How can we expect the gratitude of society when we increasingly reject any obligation or responsibility toward it, when we barricade ourselves within our privileged "academic community" and play private games among ourselves?

I recently visited a professor of literature at a respected Eastern university. While we were discussing the hiring of a new faculty member he commented with satisfaction on the publication record of his younger colleague. "Yes," I responded, "but what about his teaching?" His eyes widened in surprise. "Who cares about his teaching?" he replied impatiently and without a trace of irony. "This isn't a teaching institution—this is a *quality* university." That attitude is not uncommon. In fact the more prestigious the university, the more dominant such attitudes are likely to be. Everyone gives lip service to "excellence in teaching" (after all, students and their tuition are necessary evils), but the bottom line is that professors who publish profusely get tenure, and those who do not get fired.

There is certainly nothing wrong with sincere scholarship, and it is not unreasonable to recruit faculty who pursue it actively, particularly for graduate programs. But our primary endeavor should not be cranking out esoteric trivia or running to conventions to posture at each other. Scholars with anything significant to contribute to human knowledge are likely to do so with minimal institutional pressure. The "research" craze among the humanities disciplines began some decades ago with what we perceived as the challenge of the natural sciences. Never mind that publishing the results of a chemical experiment is not even remotely parallel to composing an essay on literary theory. We felt that we had to keep up with the Joneses who were getting so much publicity over in the science labs. (Look Ma! We're doing "research" too!) We continue doing it for the same reason that hospitals acquire expensive medical equipment they do not need: prestige, both personal and institutional—a remarkably shallow motive for those who claim such depth and sophistication. We have to do it for the simple reason that everyone else is doing it. Ironically it is primarily the faculty itself which is creating the pressure to publish, and since no one seems capable of doing anything about it, the publication mania has escalated from the merely ridiculous to the utterly absurd. Resentment among faculty members is widespread, particularly among the younger, untenured professors who bear most of the burden. But in an era when flocks of surplus Ph.D.'s man the nation's taxicabs, fear for one's reputation among colleagues, not to mention one's job, has strangled open criticism. Meanwhile, publishing has been established as the basis of the faculty rewards system, and students have become little more than irksome distractions.

The pursuit of knowledge is and should remain a major function of the university, including the humanities divisions, but the current publishing frenzy has little to do with an honest pursuit of knowledge. The majority do not publish because they have something to say. They look for something to say because they have to publish, and the difference—to borrow a phrase from Mark Twain—is like the difference between lightning and the lightning bug. We are stuffing our libraries with endless reformulations of the obvious and trivial. Nobody needs it, nobody reads it, and it is not surprising that society is growing reluctant to pay for it. If we can—and we must—put scholarship back into reasonable perspective, it will regain the honor and respect which true scholarship deserves. More to the point, it will become an adjunct function to the proper, primary goal of the university, which is the molding of young minds.

But how is all this to be accomplished? How do we go about changing the fundamental nature of our college faculties? The solution to the problem, if one is possible, will be complex and gradual. The most immediate and obvious necessity is to break the cycle of academic inbreeding. (What other enterprise is run solely by those who are its own product?) We could do so simply by ceasing to regard publications as the sole basis for faculty hiring, and instead giving equal weight to leadership experience in the society at large. In other words, institutions should actively recruit qualified individuals who have served for some time in nonacademic positions. At the same time we could encourage our present humanities faculties to acquaint themselves with America's mainstream reality by offering sabbatical leaves, not just for scholarly research, but for practical service in government, business, charity, or the like. The purpose of these policies would not be to turn the faculty into businessmen, but to help them establish connections between the abstract and the concrete, between intellect and reality, that is, to develop an engaged, dynamic, and useful intellectualism in America's colleges and universities. Socrates, Goethe, and even Thomas Jefferson were actively and effectively involved in the leadership of their societies. That intellectualism and practical action are fundamentally incompatible is a myth which history constantly disproves.

Even these modest changes will not be possible, however, until we overcome the current crises of finances and falling enrollments. It will be difficult to tempt qualified people into academe if we can offer them only a fraction of their present salaries, and the survival panic that has become a permanent state for so many college professors discourages even minor policy changes. Those perched precariously on the gunwales tend to shout down any suggestion of movement on the boat. Ironically the financial state of most institutions could be improved simply by the faculty demanding it. We are so accustomed to accepting the crumbs thrown our way that our grumbling is rarely heard beyond institutional walls. Professors should write angry letters to their congressmen, to their alumni, to the local newspaper. They should speak to church groups, civic clubs—anybody and everybody who will listen if told the truth about the slow-motion disaster which is overtaking American education.

The problem of demographics is an intractable one. We cannot create a greater college-age population overnight. We *can* reduce the number of institutions competing for students, however, and I only wish we had the moral courage to do so. Some small colleges have already failed. Others will fail in the next few years. Many more unquestionably should, but will not, because of the amoral instinct for self-preservation which has created the concept of a "diploma for sale"—graduation virtually guaranteed if you (or your father) can write well enough to sign a tuition check. If we insist on preserving every existing faculty position at whatever cost to educational standards, then there is indeed little hope for the future, either of the profession or of American society.

On the other hand, if we could reduce the number of colleges and universities to correspond to the drop in qualified students, we could then gradually reestablish reasonable entrance requirements. This in itself would go a long way toward improving the quality of primary and secondary education in America (just as our lowering of requirements contributed to its decline) by putting community pressure—and support—behind local schools to prepare their students to meet tougher standards.

Am I really asking my colleagues to commit professional suicide and accept the demise of their own institutions? Yes. Either that or convert them into vocational or junior colleges which could offer the remedial education now provided only out of exasperated necessity, and thus poorly. If we really possess the ethical superiority we like to imagine, then we must take such steps. And if we are truly of superior intelligence and understanding, then we should be able to survive quite well outside of academe. In fact many of us would make more valuable contributions in an alternative profession—and fall asleep at night with the unaccustomed sense of having done something honest and useful. Better yet, our colleagues who remain in the profession would have a chance to acquire that same satisfaction. The simple truth is that there are far too many of us, and the healthiest thing we could do for our profession is to trim away some of our sickly institutions.

With such changes accomplished, America's colleges and universities could institute real reforms. We might then begin to regain the respect and support of a nation which is abandoning us because we have abandoned it. Of course, bringing about positive change will require decisiveness and courage. It will require strong, effective leadership within the academy itself—and that remains the major stumbling block to optimism.

Where Have All the Flowers Gone?
An Eschatological Time-Motion Study of the Higher Learning and Other Desert Plants

Theodore D. Nordenhaug

South of Eden

If institutions did not already exist, human beings would invent them. Human inventiveness being what it is, we would very likely invent them to become just what they are now. But the point is academic, here South of Eden where institutions already exist.

They exist in order to give enough social definition to a human activity so that participants may then engage in the activity without being continually distracted by having to make arrangements for engaging in it. Institutions work well when they draw the least possible attention to themselves as institutions. They work badly when they begin to drain off energy from the activity they were designed to promote by drawing constant attention to the means they use to promote it.

For example, people who for one reason or another find their attention continually drawn to the fact that they are married are more likely to divorce than those who manage to keep their reflections on this fact to a minimum. The reason is that one cannot reflect on particular institutional arrangements without also reflecting on ways to improve them—at least one cannot in the modern world. And having thought of possibilities for improving them, one then becomes dissatisfied when things fail to improve, as they almost always do, when measured against the infinitude of possible improvements. That is why the Almighty in his provident wisdom forbade the first pair in the garden to taste of the fruit of the Tree of the Knowledge of Good and Evil, the Edenic ancestor of the Tree of the Consciousness of Possible Improvements, which is indigenous to North America.

Having nevertheless tasted the fruit of the Tree, most people instinctively feel—albeit too late—that they need to maintain some preserve of total unconsciousness to have any chance at life at all. So they will generally go to great lengths to avoid thinking, and especially to avoid thinking directly about the institutions that have some immediate relation to their lives. This circumstance helps institutions work. Unfortunately, however—and this is also a part of the bitter legacy of the first pair to us—the fall from innocence shows itself in how little freedom we have to choose the things that force their attentions on our attention.

South of Eden institutions do not work very well at all. So when an institution with some immediate claim on us begins to fail us, be it a marriage, a school, a workplace, a church, or a government, it then inevitably calls itself to our attention. Then we have a hard choice: either to ignore its persistent demand to be thought about, or to think about it. *Tertium non datur.* If we choose the former course we may stumble down the psycho path of repression that ends in the slough of therapy. If we choose the latter, our course may lead us *in extremis* to philosophy, theology, and thence to eschatology.

Most people do not relish these extremes and so try to mix a little repression with a little thinking. This pragmatic approach works fairly well, but only when the failure of the institution is not utter.

Apocalypse Later

In any event, anyone who persists in thinking about an institution and its prospects will eventually be drawn into eschatology. Eschatology studies the last things.

These pages contain the reflections, not altogether random, of a practicing eschatologist living in Macon, Georgia. It is only fair to warn the reader that the eschatologist is not licensed to practice. So the possibility cannot be excluded that what is said here is pure quackery. The eschatologist himself is not disturbed by this charge, however. For he expects to draw his readers only from among those who, having exhausted all other remedies, are desperate enough to try anything. The first rule of eschatological thought (or quackery) is to do no harm. Since eschatology is a study of the terminal by the terminal for the terminal, in the sense in which degrees and patients are said to be terminal, the eschatologist feels certain that he can comply with the one ethical absolute of his profession. (This does not mean that the eschatologist would not like to do harm, if he could. It merely means that he thinks that given the present state of things he cannot in fact do any.)

The novelist, Walker Percy, has observed that a depressed commuter on a train feels better when he reads a book about a depressed commuter on a train. Percy does not say whether the commuter's depression is increased when the train is stalled in a tunnel. At any rate, eschatology is for those who know that the train is not moving. It aims to make them feel better.

The philosopher, F. H. Bradley, once defined philosophy as giving bad reasons for what we believe on instinct. Eschatology gives no reasons for what it believes on instinct. That is largely because the instinct in question is the sense of smell.

These reflections might have been about any institution in contemporary life, say an Oldsmobile dealership, the First National Bank, the First Baptist Church, or a school of cosmetology. As it happens, however, they relate in one way or another to what Veblen called "the higher learning" in America, and sometimes to a particular endeavor within it called "the liberal arts." The reader might have discovered this without being told. Nonetheless it was best to mention it, since eschatology proceeds without much explicit discussion of the things it is discussing, and avoids all definition, inasmuch as it denies any present capacity to give real definition to things.

Still, even an eschatologist may occasionally permit himself a definitive remark. Liberal education, as its name implies, is liberating. The question is what it liberates one from and for. The answer is that it liberates one to practice eschatology by liberating one from the fear of said practice. This is quite in keeping with more traditional conceptions of its aim as liberating the mind from the bondage of the present, that is, that which presents itself whether we like it or not. Liberal education used to liberate by initiating people into the riches of the cultural heritage. That it can no longer do this without the aid of eschatological reflection is hardly the fault of eschatology.

Authentic eschatological reflection is to be sharply distinguished from traditional doomsaying. For one thing traditional apocalypticism makes forecasts, whereas a true eschatologist works mostly by hindcasts. For another, the traditional forms are objective, concerning themselves with the last things in a manner appropriate to a lead story on the network evening newscasts: "Good evening. CBS News has learned that the world is expected to end at 8:32 p.m., Eastern Standard Time. CBS will stay on the air to bring you live, up to the moment coverage on these fast-breaking events. For more on the story we now switch you to Dan Rather standing by in Armageddon. . . ." And so on. The true eschatology, being existential, never makes the news.

Traditional doomcasts appear in a religious and a secular form. The important difference is that in the former God is in charge of the final disposition, whereas in the latter man is. The popular religious apocalypses depart from one of the many literal readings of the Bible, usually with heavy emphasis on the book of Revelation, and try to decode contemporary world events in terms of it. Often they do a better job than the CBS Evening News. Often they don't. Their main interest is to proclaim the vengeance of God upon those who have not had the foresight to become righteous by accepting the warnings of the lavender-shirt evangelists and by contributing generously to the Seventh Seal Radio Hour of America. They are of interest mainly as a unique American art form.

The secular apocalypticism departs from the various topical crises of our age. It makes projections, draws graphs, and above all, invents scenarios. It deals mostly in fact-futures, which are closely related to copper-futures and soybean-futures, which in turn are thought to be essentially related to people-futures. It can center on the arms-race and the bomb, the population explosion, the natural resource and energy crises, the heat death of the planet or the universe, and the decline in faculty purchasing power. Or it may focus on all of them together. It conjures visions of a barren world without K-Marts, Buicks, "The Gong Show," McDonald's, and Olivia Newton-John records, and so confronts people poignantly with the question whether there will be enough civilization in the future to make life worth living. It is of interest as a science form, since it is data-based.

The true appeal of both to their practitioners is that they meet the need of an alienated humanity to see things ended, and so with one's own alienation, which consists fundamentally in the fact that one has become a thing to oneself, and so secretly wants to be ended. Religious apocalypses offer judgment, finality, and the secret solace of cathartic fire and brimstone. That is why the latter-day prophets who set a date for the end of the world always find customers who are eager to join the righteous remnant to wait for it on a mountain in Arkansas. Similarly the secular scenarios offer judgment, finality, and the secret solace of cathartic megadeaths, fallout, silent springs, and closing circles. That is why they too have their following, who hope to become a righteous remnant in a fallout shelter or in an energy self-sufficient geodesic dome in the Northwoods of Maine.

The authentic eschatology has no reason to doubt that the world will end sooner or later, and that it will probably end sooner rather than later. If the second law of thermodynamics doesn't get us, then the Whore of Babylon certainly will. So it does not deny that one or another of the scenarios, or maybe even all of them, may come true. But objective mega-catastrophe is not of ultimate interest to an eschatologist who knows his craft. His thoughts are more likely to be drawn to the man who once predicted that the world would end in the year 2007 and was run over by an Amoco tanker truck that very afternoon.

Being about the present rather than the future, and being existential rather than objective, authentic eschatology is more about life than death. For this reason it is bleaker than traditional apocalypticism. It teaches how everlastingly the last things last, once one realizes that one is already surrounded by them. In so doing it takes all the fun out of the apocalypse.

Franz Kafka was one of the more prescient eschatologists of our century. He once addressed this gruesome observation to his diary: "The end of the world will not come on the last day, but the day after that." In the stagnant spiritual air mass that pressed down on *Mitteleu-ropa* in the decaying Austro-Hungarian Empire, Kafka sniffed the truth about twentieth century institutional life: the fact that something has ended does not suffice to stop it. His dark oracle refers us to a world in which men have lived up all their meanings without being able to live beyond them. It is a world of those who merely survive. It is also the world of "the higher learning."

The meanings that once animated it have been used up, lived up, exhausted. It has lost too much blood. The frantic efforts to transfuse it by mission statements and declarations of purpose come too late. They cannot save it. Institutions, like people, seek purpose only when they have none. Never yet has the sixth draft of a committee's statement of purpose restored aims to the aimless. Nor the seventh. It is even cruel to hold out hope to the aimless in this way.

Who can pretend to be about the business of seeking and imparting wisdom, or even knowledge, or anything, when he is alone in his office with a stack of sixty essays on *Macbeth*, poring over the condensed version of the *Cliff Notes* version of "Out, out, brief candle," where life is full of sound and furry, signifying what?—A spelling error? Illiteracy? F? D-? Failure of the mission? What was it then? If it failed, we ought to be able to say what failed. Let's make it C-.

Does anyone still find it possible to believe? Forget about what one overhears oneself saying in a committee meeting. The issue is belief! And Something to believe in! An end! A purpose! A point! A *telos*! Or does analysis block off every avenue to conviction? And does then the energy spent refusing to engage in analysis drain every hope that life shall return to this barren mindscape? Is it then the paycheck that keeps this machinery going? It keeps Henry Ford's factory going. Can it also keep his academy going? Without belief?

Apparently, Franz, you were right.

Students pay their tuition and fees. Bells ring. Lectures commence. Bells ring. Lectures stop. Testing occurs. Grading happens. Computers print numbers. Credit hours and G.P.A.'s are faithfully recorded. The faculty meets. Committees meet. They agree to meet again. Subcommittees are appointed. Publications are published. Government grants are received. Policies are set in motion. Policies are reviewed. Planning takes place. Things are administered.

There is something eerie about this machinery humming on, like a transformer out in the wilderness. Who tends it? People don't want to think about that. They say it's Kafka-esque. That is why, when they think about it, people decide that it is best not to think about it. So they stop thinking about it.

There are, to be sure, enough distractions. One way not to think about it is to dabble in academic apocalypticism, which has the signal virtue of not being academic. Everyone knows that this is to be the Darwinian decade for the overbuilt American education industry. On the last day the topic of the day is survival to the day after that. Will the righteous remnant also be the fittest? So what if the two images do not cohere? Mixing our metaphors is a helpful distraction. For who wants to deal with that other question, the unspoken and unspeakable question: What if, against all odds, we do survive? What then? What if the apocalypse is later? What then?

No one wants to get into that question at all, Franz, no one at all. It is the most academic of questions.

On the Last Day

Herzog, another practitioner of eschatology, once proclaimed that what this country needs is a good five-cent synthesis. This eschatologist thinks it also needs a good theory of decadence. The price is no object. Such a theory will explain how it is that institutions can come to such a pass that their sole consuming interest is to survive. It will then proceed to demonstrate that the universe really does have a moral direction after all, so that any institution whose sole consuming interest is to survive, won't: it doesn't deserve to.

Someday there will be such a theory. And it will establish the priority of the question "Survival for what?" over the question of survival.

Meanwhile in the absence of such a theory, the eschatologist is condemned to survival in the sense in which the obituary says: "The deceased is survived by his spouse."

The exact date when anything worth calling education deceased, leaving the eschatologist behind as its survivor, cannot be fixed with certainty. But an eschatologist cannot help speculating on when the mortal remains came to be interred in the gigantic mausoleum of "the higher learning," particularly since he has discovered that he has the misfortune to have been interred with them.

On those days when the eschatologist tries to take a broad view of history, he suspects that education may have ended, for all practical purposes, when Francis Bacon announced that "knowledge is power," thereby overturning the long-standing view that in the best case knowledge was only knowledge, that in the worst case it was not much of anything at all, and that in any case wisdom was better, and that wisdom consisted to a large extent of knowing something about the limits of knowledge and power.

At other times the eschatologist thinks that education met its end in the great explosion. Not the one in Hiroshima in 1945, for that was only a sympathetic explosion touched off by the great knowledge explosion. When the higher learning blew up it was a spectacle as poignant to anyone with the slightest feeling for history as the fate of the Parthenon when the Turks hit upon the idea—was it about the time of Francis Bacon?—of using it as a powder magazine. Many have discussed the event, but none better than John Lukacs in *The Passing of the Modern Age*:

> Beyond the relationship of teachers and students there looms the monstrous problem of the dissolution of learning among teachers and potential teachers, among the purveyors of learning itself. This problem has become monstrous because of its dimensions. The inflation of society includes the inflation of the world of teachers and scholars. Their professional advancement habitually depends upon publications. These are now so numerous that sometimes more than one half of the books and journals in respectable libraries may consist of publications of the last fifteen or twenty years. There exist harebrained men and women who hail this kind of thing as the Knowledge Explosion, whereas it is nothing less than the cancerous dissolution of learning. Until very recently scholars had been plagued by a scarcity of printed materials relevant to their disciplines. Suddenly the very opposite has happened. The best of them struggle as they are snowed under by printed matter, while the weaker ones let their span of attention contract to the point of intellectual corruption.
>
> The dissolution of learning is an essential part of a general breakdown of communications. I think it was Matthew Arnold who said that the end of the Middle

Ages came with the development of communications. The end of the Modern Age comes with their breakdown, which means, too, the increasing loneliness of people, very much including young people, surrounded though they are by more people than ever before.

This is a great paradox: this enormous development of external communications at the same time with the breaking down of the interior ones. And there is another great paradox: the superficially revolutionary character of our times, beneath which we may detect extraordinary extents of intellectual stagnation. Probably the latter, too, has much to do with the contracting attention-span and with the breakdown of interior communications: superficially we can receive, and dismiss, a fantastic amount of flickering images and messages while we are, more than often unconsciously, bored with their essential sameness.[1]

At yet other times it seems to the eschatologist that education may have ended with the advent of mass man at the turn of the century or thereabouts, the so-called "vertical invasion of the Barbarians," who had to be absorbed into all kinds of civilized institutions that simply were not ready for them, and so were left looking like a makeshift Red Cross aid-station after a Guatemalan revolution.

Sometimes when the eschatologist is in a more jingoistic mood, he suspects it may have ended the day the Russians sent Sputnik into orbit and a great clamor arose in the land over the prospect of an electronic Soviet eye gazing down through the ionosphere into the empty, uneducated minds of Americans, whose minds were empty, of course, because they had lost the race to be the first to build a similar eye to gaze into the minds of the Russians, which, in turn, would have been empty if the Americans had won. At any rate the superiority of the Soviet educational system was henceforward clear even to empty-headed Americans, who immediately set to work with American know-how to crank up Henry Ford's assembly line as the quickest, most efficient way to fill up their empty minds with an education that

---

[1]John Lukacs, *The Passing of the Modern Age* (New York: Harper and Row, 1970), pp. 110-11.

would enable them to leave the planet before anyone else beat them to it. The expertness produced by the great higher teaching machine soon enabled the Americans to play golf on the moon. At the same time, it made the prospect of leaving the planet attractive even to duffers, as a plume of stupefaction wafted aloft from the chimneys of the great learning factories and settled heavily over the cool, green hills of earth. As Christopher Lasch describes the result:

> People increasingly find themselves unable to use language with ease and precision, to recall the basic facts of their country's history, to make logical deductions, to understand any but the most rudimentary written texts, or even to grasp their constitutional rights. The conversion of popular traditions of self-reliance into esoteric knowledge administered by experts encourages a belief that ordinary competence in almost any field, even the art of self-government, lies beyond the reach of the layman. Standards of teaching decline, the victims of poor teaching come to share the expert's low opinion of their capacities, and the teaching profession complains of unteachable students.[2]

Finally, the eschatologist, growing weary of theories, is content to suppose that education ended on the day absolutely everyone including the Grand Kleagle of the Ku Klux Klan, the Black Panthers, world-weary Jewish intellectuals, and Sears & Roebuck executives had come to believe in "the higher learning" as the ticket window for the American Dream, now playing in Pan-A-Vision, and so created degrees of life, an arrangement celebrated in the TV ad where a greasy functionary in an employment service tells honest Abe Lincoln: "You ain't goin' nowhere without that sheepskin, fella!"

The idea of living by degrees increased the kinds of creatures who need sheepskins in order to exist to two: sheep and Americans. Having a competitor for his skin at first worked a hardship on the sheep. But American know-how contrived to produce artificial sheepskins, so that now the economics of the thing works rather to the detriment of the Americans. The sheep, whose attachment to his skin was always rooted in a certain natural logic, can now keep his skin; the hapless

---

[2]Christopher Lasch, *The Culture of Narcissism* (New York: Norton, 1978), p. 128.

American cannot. Resentment being what it is, however, one day the Americans will subject the wooly sheep to higher learning. And then on some far-off hillside in a not so far-off future, as the curfew tolls the knell of a parting day, a sheepish Ph.D. in human ethology may *ewe*phonically bleat to her flock: "You ain't goin' nowhere without that peopleskin, lambchop!"

At any rate, the old human learning is gone. Did it die of old age? Or did it succumb to an iatrogenic illness, an overdose of attention from all the doctors who tried to save it? Or was the cause of death an idiopathic disease? "Idiopathic" is the medical term that doctors use when they don't know what the hell you've got: "I'm sorry to tell you that you have idiopathic softening of the brain. There is no cure at the moment, but new things come out every day. Besides, with rest and especially no strenuous reflection, you can live for quite a while. I'm afraid you'll have to give up eschatology though."

Eschatologists are not coroners. So it is not their job to fix the time and exact cause of death. It is enough that they know a corpse when they see one. Eschatologists are, like other people, just survivors. They know only that they live after the great misadventure, whatever it was and whenever it was. And they differ from noneschatological survivors only in supposing that they know where they are and what time it is. Time, they know, stands still in the higher mausoleum.

In the Snack Bar of a well-known liberal arts college there are two clocks. The one in the kitchen runs normally; the other, in the main dining area has stopped. As people order lunch they can glance at the kitchen clock and see that the burgers and fries are reassuringly immersed in normal, greasy Newtonian time. But when the customers take their trays into the main dining area, only the stopped clock will be easily visible. It says ll:20. The faculty's table is almost directly under it.

Nearly every day some faculty member will gaze up absently from a Styrofoam coffee cup or a Styrofoam conversation, and exclaim with a start, "That clock cannot be right!" or "They really ought to get that damned thing fixed!" He will then strain to see the clock in the kitchen, or check his wristwatch. Reassured by this that time has indeed moved on in his absence, the faculty member will mutter a few departing pleasantries and go about his afternoon chores.

This little ritual is deceiving, however. Eschatologists know that the stopped clock keeps perfect time. It is always ll:20, Eschatological

Standard Time, on the last day. Yesterday, which was the last day, the clock said ll:20. And tomorrow, which will also be the last day, the clock will also say ll:20.

For skeptics, who do not believe in the power of symbols, there are other ways to confirm the time.

It was on the last day that the same liberal arts college whose clock had stopped over the faculty wanted to consider reforming its curriculum and appointed a Steering Committee with many subcommittees, one of which was unblinkingly called the Cultural Heritage Subcommittee. On the last day, how else could one propose to get at the cultural heritage in a liberal arts college except by forming a subcommittee? The cultural heritage *is* a subcommittee.

It was on the last day some years later when the curriculum committee of the same college was making its decisions mainly by the precedent of appealing to the course descriptions in the catalogues of other colleges and universities. Those other colleges and universities had no doubt established their course offerings by appealing to the catalogues of yet other colleges and universities, who, in turn, had established their curriculum by appealing. . . . "Barbarism," says Ortega, "is the absence of standards to which appeals can be made."

It was on the last day that the same college became concerned to provide a growth environment for the students. So the student development office busied itself with transplanting the students who had just arrived from their hydroponic homes by carefully testing them for personality. It then repotted them in the rich, nutritious soil of the higher greenhouse, where student life is climate-controlled and kept at a constant temperature the year round, and where playing pinball is a growth-experience, and walking with a girl in the moonlight is a growth-experience, and painting one's room is a growth-experience, and kissing a girl in the moonlight is a growth-experience, and conjugating Spanish verbs is a growth-experience, and breaking up in daylight with the girl one kissed in moonlight is a growth-experience, and joining a sorority is a growth-experience, and reading that the unexamined life is not worth living is a growth-experience, and crying softly because one has been kissed in the moonlight and broken up with in daylight is a growth-experience, and doing calculus problems is a growth-experience. And why then does this nurturing environment, the best that anyone could wish for, somehow gives one the feeling that it is like being boiled to death in a vat of marshmallows? Why does this greenhouse somehow make one want to side with Oscar in *The Tin Drum* who at the age of four in another time and place took a good look at all the growth opportunities in the growing Third Reich and then refused, flatly refused, to grow, preferring instead to become a midget drumming his way through war-crazed Germany from Danzig to the Atlantic Wall? Does it have something to do with the moist, stifling air of the greenhouse, where it is hard for humans to breathe? And will death too become a significant growth-experience? In any case, growth grows like kudzu on the last day. Someday even eschatology may provide a significant growth-experience.

It was on the last day that a professional organization in the humanities held a conference whose entire program contained not a single paper in the humanities. It focused instead on ways to increase enrollments in humanities, and brainstorming ways to increase administrative backing for humanities programs. The rationale was that only by acquiring these skills could humanists save the humanities from imminent death. The featured plenary session of the conference was entitled: "A Workshop on Workshops."

It was on the last day that insurance companies discovered that there was a new lucrative market in selling malpractice insurance to colleges and universities.

It was on the last day that the quantity of publication became the main means of advancement in the academy, so that publication became an end in itself, and the question of what was to be published an afterthought. People then published—publications. In response to this situation, which had created a tremendous traffic jam for the professional journals, a compassionate problem-solver invented a journal that publishes directly on microfilm. It is called the *Philosophy Research Archives.* It enables the scholar not only to gain his publication credits more rapidly but it also makes him instantaneously historical. One can write directly for the ages, without having to concern oneself about a contemporary readership. On the last day no one reads what one writes anyway.

It was on the last day that the psychology department in a prestigious California university hired a professional gag-writer to spice up the lectures of faculty members so they could get even more laughs. Even Cardinal Newman is laughing.

It was on the last day that a state univerity in Ohio offered a course in riding a roller coaster for two hours credit. It was on the last day that students enrolled in it at a cost of sixty-five dollars, when they could have purchased the same number of roller coaster rides for fifteen dollars, without having to write a paper.

It was on the last day that an institution of higher learning in Kentucky decided to stuff one hundred balloons with offers of a scholarship to the finder, and so threw education to the prevailing winds.

It was on the last day that the American Philosophical Association discovered that there might be a whole new field of employment for its members in teaching philosophy to children in the primary grades.

It was, in sum, the last day when the only question on the minds of the denizens of the higher learning in America was how to survive, and nobody was asking, "Survival for what?"

On the last day mankind had more knowledge at its disposal than in all previous ages put together, and the world was less intelligible than ever before.

On the last day biologists made babies in test tubes, and men and women submerged themselves in hot tubs and did all manner of things to one another's increasingly superfluous genitals.

On the last day sincere, compassionate liberals carried picket signs and wrote letters to the editor and lobbied against capital punishment. On the last day the very same people fought with equal sincerity for abortion as a natural right of woman.

On the last day sincere, compassionate conservatives carried picket signs and wrote letters to the editor and lobbied for the right to life and tried to outlaw abortion. On the last day the very same sincere people bought Gary Gilmore T-shirts and cheered when he was shot by the state of Utah.

On the last day the liberals acted as if abortion would eliminate the need for capital punishment, and the conservatives acted as if capital punishment were a deterrent to abortion.

On the last day nearly everything was a matter of life and death, and the difference between life and death was no longer clear.

On the last day when a whole race of people was being exterminated in Cambodia, people were deeply fascinated by the question, "Who shot J.R.?"

On the last day men had more toys and means of amusement at their disposal than in all previous history, and they were bored comatose.

On the last day on a television program called "Real People" a man drank a glass of beer while standing on his head. The studio audience cheered itself hoarse. Was it ecstatic because it had at long last discovered what real people are supposed to do?

On the last day many women liberated themselves so that they could participate fully in the glamor of real work and become advertising executives and public relations consultants.

On the last day many males liberated themselves by leaving their glamorous jobs as advertising executives and public relations consultants and came out of the closet to live with their own kind as poets in San Francisco.

On the last day man had more means for solving his problems than in all previous ages put together, and he became a problem to himself. He once tried a final solution. Next time it may really be final.

On the last day there was more enlightened social concern than ever before, and more programs to aid the old, the poor, the sick, and the mentally ill than in all the previous ages of the world put together, and people murdered one another in plain sight of their neighbors who merely watched.

On the last day when men presided over the most marvelous machinery of communication, with television, satellites, and radio telescopes, so that they could send messages instantaneously around the globe as well as to remote galaxies, and search deep space for intelligent life forms, they could think of little to say to their wives and children and were preoccupied with getting in touch with their own feelings.

On the last day people used their car bumpers to communicate their deepest thoughts. Some said: "I found it." Others said: "I never lost it."

On the last day when people talked most about growth and self-realization they sired a race of whining emotional pygmies.

On the last day when many were irate at the government for not allowing prayer in the schools, no one prayed for the schools.

And on the last day when an urgent, emergency meeting of educators from around the globe should have been in session at the United Nations to bring the vast resources of modern learning to bear on the paradoxes and confusions of the last day, the educators went about their business as usual, seeking promotions, getting grants, complaining about administrative incompetence and student stupidity, bemoaning the decline in their purchasing power, and between times taught psychopathology, and the decline of the Roman Empire, and the decline of the novel, and management as if nothing were amiss at all, as if it were not the last day, but just another ordinary day in the civilized world that was progressing through data-banks, efficiency studies, planning, and integrated circuits toward the reestablishment of Eden on earth.

The educators acted for all the world as if they still believed something. But the eschatologist hadn't a clue as to what it might be.

When the eschatologist (or quack) had hammered out these bizarre thoughts on his typewriter, he left his office and trudged down to the Snack Bar through the drizzle to perk up his spirits with a cup of coffee. As he sat down in the booth, he happened to glance up at the clock. It was exactly 11:20.

Istanbul Was Constantinople

Some sociologist will no doubt arise to challenge this eschatology by pointing out that we are simply dealing with the normal phenomena of social change: the adaptation of an institution to changing societal conditions that require it to take on new functions. Such change, our sociologist will patiently explain, often produces "cultural lag," a phenomenon more recently dramatized for popular consumption as "future shock," which can be exemplified, among other ways, in alienated ruminations on the last things. For his part, the eschatologist is eager to be consoled as soon as he can get a microfilm copy of the sociologist's data-base and verify for himself that there is hard statistical evidence that the higher learning has a future worth going into shock over.

Meanwhile he has no doubt at all that colleges and universities operate under vastly changed conditions with "new" students and "new" faculty who perform "new" functions. It is, for example, a new function for the higher learning in America to keep large numbers of skill-less young people off a glutted labor market. It is also a new function for the higher learning to operate like a K-Mart, with blue light specials on social work or journalism or management or pre-med, or whatever the latest market research predicts will bring the customers running in a given year. It is also a new function for the higher learning to assume the functions of the lower, either by trying to teach large numbers of eighteen year olds, with twelve years of schooling already behind them, to read and write; or, failing that, to emulate whatever the lower learning did for them by arranging to transmit the cultural heritage in such a manner that students need not be subjected to the cultural lag of having to acquire these antiquated habits.

There was once another institution that assumed a new function. In 1453 when the Turks took Constantinople they stabled their horses in St. Sophia's Basilica. Now let us assume—purely as a sociological *Gedankenexperiment*—that this new function of the great church persisted for several Turkish generations, while, at the same time by reason of linguistic inertia, the old name of St. Sophia's Basilica was retained. Why then, if a Turkish sociologist is asked to explain the purpose of the Basilica, will he not state in no uncertain terms that a basilica is a horse stable, as any fool of an infidel can plainly see? And if the infidel is stubborn and professes to doubt this account of the matter, then surely the Turkish sociologist will conduct him to St. Sophia's church and subject him to the empirical data. After seeing and smelling, and perhaps even stepping in the new function, not even the stubbornest infidel can continue to doubt that it is the primary end of a basilica to be connected with the business end of a horse.

The affable Turkish sociologist will, of course, be happy to discuss relevant questions, such as whether basilicas are the best conceivable stables, and whether one might not expect improvements in the state of the art of stable building, so to speak, and design more efficient arrangements in the future. Indeed, even the ordinary Turkish stable-boys, who know nothing of sociology, have a great many ideas for improving the stable, most of which naturally center on making life easier for Turkish stableboys.

But, improvements or no improvements, it would be as absurd to try to deny that a basilica is a place to stable horses as to don the vestments and say an equine mass in the name of the Father, the Son and the Holy Ghost.

Clearly there are new functions for basilicas just as there are for higher education.

The eschatologist is not as distressed by the existence of the new functions as he is by the peculiar tendency of the Turkish language to identify the new functions with the old. Turkish grammar would not disturb him as much if it permitted one to say: "The Basilica of the infidels has fallen and we have replaced it with something useful and good and distinctively Turkish, namely a stable." For that could at least be discussed. But there is no way to say any such thing in Turkish or even to hint at it. Instead Turks use the old names of things for new functions, so that to the Turkish mind a basilica *is* a horse stable, cannot possibly be anything other than a horse stable, and never really was anything other than a mere structure awaiting the arrival of progressive Turks so it could then be a horse stable.

The infidel eschatologist clings to his culturally laggard belief that a basilica is a basilica, and a horse stable, a horse stable. But he has no way to express this antique thought to Turks. And since there is no one else around much to talk to but Turks—indeed, some of the infidel's best friends are Turks—whenever the infidel tries to talk about the purpose of a basilica to a Turk, the Turk immediately thinks horse stable. He then looks at him with the quizzical indulgence so typical of Turks and strains into the void to match his Turkish meanings with strange terms like "the mass," and "the vestments" and "*Kyrie Eleison.*" Whereupon he can only draw the conclusion that this must be some primitive infidel way of referring to saddles and bridles and shovels and horses and horse manure and smells and flies and the other various and sundry accoutrements of Turkish stabledom.

The eschatologist recalls the observation of Bishop Butler that "each thing is what it is, and not another thing." His truism is the plainest of falsisms in Turkish, where each thing is precisely what it is not, and nothing is ever itself.

In Istanbul intelligence *is* a certain score on a test. In Istanbul knowing something *is* getting a certain grade on an exam, and scholastic achievement *is* a grade point average. In Istanbul all qualities are quantities. In Istanbul teaching *is* giving a course, and learning *is* taking it. In Istanbul getting an education *is* collecting a certian number of courses on a transcript. In Istanbul the common vocabulary of the faculty *is* exhausted by words such as "degrees," "courses," "credit hours," "salary," "tenure," "promotion," and there is no public language to express ideas and consequently no ideas. And in Istanbul because of the manifest *isness* of all these things no one even imagines that an institution of learning might be or has ever been anything else.

As he contemplates the bustling life of Istanbul, the eschatologist falls into deep melancholy over the plight of the Turkish stableboys. He wonders whether they ever wonder, even fleetingly, as they shovel out the stable in the morning, about the misty inaccessible and inexpressible un-Turkish past of St. Sophia's church. But he suspects that any hint of Turkish astonishment will be quickly driven from a stable

Turkish mind by the equestrian thought that horse stables are absolutely essential in Istanbul, and that even though shoveling out the stable in the morning is not the most pleasant of jobs, it is, after all, a living, an important social function, a profession, and, above all, a stableboy's thing. And he suspects that whatever few suspicions a stableboy who is doing his thing may entertain about the past activities of the Basilica, his Turkish instincts tell him that it very likely contained no provision for his thing. And so shaking off these wispy musings, a Turkish stableboy will face Mecca, say his morning prayers, and then—Allah is great and Mohamet is his only prophet!—go right on shoveling.

How should it be otherwise in Istanbul which is, after all, not Constantinople?

The Fact of Mary Lou Smith

It should be clear that the predicament of the eschatologist is not due to the fact that he has overlooked the pertinent facts. It is a fact that Turkish stables are housed in what were once basilicas. It is a fact that Turkish stables are needed in Turkish societies. It is a fact that Turkish sociologists can prove that the above are facts. It is further a fact that these facts, in all of their gooey factuality, immobilize the eschatologist, so that he gazes at them as the old battered, now limbless statue of St. Sophia must gaze down upon the horses in her church and at the busy stableboys who work there at their very factitious tasks.

The predicament of the eschatologist is that he is all too aware of the facts. In fact, it is precisely because he can neither repress them nor transcend them that the eschatologist was driven, very much against his own inclinations, to become an eschatologist. The fact is, moreover, that the eschatologist's difficulty has nothing to do with the innocent, inert facts themselves, but with his resistance to becoming one. The eschatologist would have preferred to be a teacher or a scholar, or both, or neither, but, at any rate, to ply some honest trade in which he would not have to be a fact among other sociological facts. The eschatologist, in fact, was willing to be almost anything rather than a fact, except perhaps a rhinoceros. And thereupon, as they say, hangs a tale.

It was from Mary Lou Smith that he first came to learn, about a decade ago, that all there was left for him to be was a fact; and that, if he didn't want to be one, then life was going to make damn sure that he wouldn't get to be anything but an eschatologist.

Mary Lou Smith was a very bright young lady. Her S.A.T. scores (both in the high six hundreds) and her immaculate high school four-point-oh(!) proved this incontestably to anyone who bothered to check. Mary Lou herself knew it to be a fact. Mary Lou was very bright because, as she also knew, she was very good with facts, the way some people are good with animals. She knew such facts, for example, as the difference between meiosis and mitosis, the names of all the presidents and their dates, that tragic heroes always had tragic flaws, the name of the capital of Uganda (and where it was!), that final 't's are silent in French, and the date of the Boxer Rebellion. She may even have known, although the eschatologist had no occasion to inquire, that Constantinople had fallen in 1453. If she did in fact know this, it is quite certain that she knew it to be a fact. For Mary Lou did not know anything that wasn't a fact. There were Social Studies I facts, American History II facts, Biology I and Biology II facts, and English Composition I, II, and III facts. There were Health facts, Algebra facts, and Geography facts. There were even Elective facts.

Mary Lou had not been in college long when the soon-to-be eschatologist had a very factual encounter with her. The event took place in a small freshman group that was reading, or so the prof hoped, Ionesco's play, *Rhinoceros*, and would then, or so the prof hoped, discuss it.

The play begins with some rather ordinary people leading their ordinary lives. Suddenly a rhinoceros lumbers down the main street of the town. One rhinoceros is, of course, not enough to distract ordinary people from doing ordinary things and talking about ordinary things in ordinary ways, so after passing mention of the fact that a rhinoceros was in the street and somebody probably ought to do something, the people go back to their ordinary tasks and their ordinary conversation. Then a second rhino appears, and it becomes a bit harder to maintain ordinariness. As the play unfolds more and more rhinoceri appear, and the discovery is made that the townspeople themselves are turning into rhinoceri. There is, for instance, a logician who, at an early stage of the play analyzes the rhinoceros-problem and establishes by unassailable syllogisms that it is of the utmost importance to determine whether the first rhinoceros that had been sighted had one horn or two. In due course the logician becomes a rhinoceros himself, but he can be clearly identified, even though all rhinoceri look more or less alike to the layman, because he keeps his bowler hat as he gallops and trumpets through the town. As more and more people join the bestial throng, it becomes harder and harder for the erstwhile ordinary people to go on in their ordinary pursuits, and they begin to feel a need to justify not becoming pachyderms. Since the justifications are pretty weak, the situation soon reverses itself, and everyone begins to rationalize changing into a rhinoceros. In the end, the "hero" of the play is the last human being left, but, far from being a moral example, he is left with wistful regrets about the ugliness of human skin and his inability to join the pachydermous masses.

The eschatologist can see now, as he writes, that the hero was just an eschatologist like himself. But at the time the eschatologist was not an eschatologist, and so had neither eschatological, nor even fancy literary points to make about the play. He was using it because he had supposed that it might be a vivid device to get the class to begin some reflections about the conformist pressures of college life and the real and urgent problems of "self-identity" that young people must confront. He had not, of course, yet reckoned with the self-identity of Mary Lou Smith.

To tell the truth, on the day of reckoning, the not-yet-eschatological professor thought the discussion was going pretty well. The students seemed reasonably interested, and when he brought up the existential question of fraternities and sororities and worked that into the discussion—rather neutrally he thought, considering his attitude toward this form of rhinoceritis—the conversation seemed to be moving in the right direction.

Mary Lou, however, as the prof had subliminally noted, had said not a word—remarkable behavior for Mary Lou who rarely missed an opportunity to contribute true facts and dispel false ones. Mary Lou was not only silent; she was in fact scowling. Indeed she had been scowling for at least fifteen minutes. Mary Lou had a very factual scowl. She had, as it turned out, cleverly baited the hook with the fact of her scowl, and patient fisherperson that she was, she now waited, knowing that sooner or later the fish would bite.

"Something bothering you, Mary Lou?" inquired the fish solicitiously.

The scowl vanished as she set the hook: "Yes, this whole thing is absolutely ridiculous, as you know" (the "as you know" was intended to cut off in advance any hope of pleading ignorance of the law before Judge Mary Lou).

"What do you mean?" said the too late suspicious fish.

Mary Lou waited several seconds for effect and then said in a calm, firm voice: "People don't really turn into rhinoceroses."

She didn't smile, and that was all she said.

The fish, now hopelessly aware of his predicament, tried a few anticlimactic wriggles, but he already knew it was no use. He suggested that one might hypothesize, just for the sake of argument, mind you, that Ionesco was using his vivid imagination to portray something important about the human condition, and that, for this reason, one ought to try to swing with the admittedly false assumption, the biological impossibility even, that people could turn into rhinos, just for the sake of argument, mind you, to see if the play might perhaps have something important to tell us.

But Mary Lou, who knew her victory was a plain fact, would have none of it. College was a place where serious-minded profs did real things with true facts, and it was most definitely not a place where a student's valuable time was to be wasted by a fuzzy teacher who couldn't distinguish a fact from a rhinoceros, not even when the fact impaled him on its sharp horn. It was certainly no place to play silly let's pretend games that Mary Lou had renounced once and for all in the second grade. (One imagines her second grade teacher passing around pledge cards in a solemn ceremony after the pledge of allegiance.)

The most remarkable aspect of the event, at least to the prof, was how quickly rhinoceritis set in among the other students who had been so freely and transcendently discussing the silliness of rhinoceritis only moments before. Several deserted shamelessly on the spot, as they had been around schools long enough to tell a winner from a loser— besides which they thought it might speed up the end of the class enough to get in a game of touch football before dinner. One or two others made feeble efforts to support the prof. But inasmuch as their basic attitudes toward profs was that, if they were not maybe narcs, it was still clearly a violation of the code for students to openly side with them—particularly when the plain facts went against them—they did not take up Mary Lou's challenge with enthusiasm. Besides they themselves had had their suspicions about this screwy discussion anyhow. It was as if Mary Lou had aroused their deepest patriotic feelings about their very factual world like Winston Churchill rallying his people for the Battle of Britain, and had said what they would have thought, if they had really wanted to think, it being a nice afternoon and all. And anyway if the prof, who had chosen this book anyhow and started the whole discussion anyhow, solely on his own say-so without consulting them, couldn't look after himself in a classroom where he and this Ionesco dude had made up all the rules, it was a plain fact that he wasn't going to get any help from them, who, at base, couldn't have cared less whether people in books turned into rhinos or kangaroos or professors, and who also couldn't have cared less about absurd theatre, which, now at least, had been shown to be in fact what its name said it was, restoring some measure of order to the cosmos.

So Mary Lou turned the whole class into rhinoceroses, who in turn stared at the teacher as if he were just one more dumb fact.

"I forgot to mention it before, but I need to leave a little early this afternoon," said the vanquished fact, surrendering with all the dignity the circumstances permitted.

Mary Lou and the professor lived in the tension of an unnegotiated truce for the rest of the quarter. There was a no man's land between them that neither dared enter. Mary Lou would mention whatever facts seemed pertinent to her on the topics under discussion, and write them down on her papers, for example, "Ionesco was a Romanian who lived in France, where he became an author of absurd plays. One of these plays is called *Rhinoceros.* The play is absurd because it is about people turning into rhinoceroses. In the first scene.... At the end, only one person is left who is not a rhinoceros. But even he wants to be one. This is absurd." Mary Lou, in short, stuck fast to the facts, and as her facts were invariably the true facts, the prof, beginning his journey to the *eschaton,* refrained from comment. For her part, Mary Lou, knowing that the power of the professor over her grade was a fact, refrained from further victories and hid her very factual opinions about the class in her heart (which consisted, of course, of a right and left auricle and a right and left ventricle and a bundle of His, and so forth). The prof went on in his incorrigible antifactual way. He was now a very familiar, if unpleasant fact. But precisely because he was a fact, she knew she would be able to endure. Needless to say, she never took any more classes from the aforesaid prof-fact, choosing instead to take biology and chemistry and sociology and history and math and other real subjects like that, where facts were facts and answers were right or wrong and many of the tests were true-false and the universe made sense. Since Mary Lou was rarely wrong about her facts, she got A's and B+'s and life was bountiful.

The prof followed her subsequent career, at a safe distance, with the kind of interest that the Pass Christian weather station takes in a hurricane churning through the Gulf of Mexico. She graduated with a very factual 3.76 average, which she had no doubt memorized to the tenth place. The prof expected that she would marry some very factitious young man, probably an actuary for an insurance company, and settle into the fact of the good life in the Oak Hills subdivision of Anytown (which had better have some oaks and some hills if it expects Mary Lou to live there), where she would keep her mind sharp by answering all the questions on the daytime quiz shows before the contestants can hit the buzzer.

The last he heard of her, she was teaching school in an Atlanta suburb. Eschatology being what it is, he can easily visualize the apocalyptic factuality of Miss Smith's third grade. There her charges will learn the facts about Bolivia and Kuala Lampur and everything will be put in its very factual place. She may even teach them the fact that Istanbul was once called Constantinople. And there will be an inevitable trip to the zoo where happy little boys and girls can see a rhinoceros in the flesh. They will all leave her care knowing the facts of life, or at least knowing, if they don't much cotton to learning many facts themselves, that if they are going to make it at all, they will have to grow up to be facts and find their niche in the unyielding appointed order where every item is either a true fact or a false one.

Are there tens of thousands of Mary Lous teaching millions of kids in the schools of the land? When the eschatologist ponders this question, as he is condemned to, he shudders. He would then, if he were a more religious man, light a candle in remembrance of what happened at Constantinople in 1453.

Job's Problem and the Job Problem

Everyone knows that schools, and especially colleges and universities, should not be teaching isolated facts to the Mary Lou Smiths of this world, even though that is mostly what they end up doing when they teach anything at all. The eschatologist would like to reflect on this discrepancy between what everybody knows and what institutions of learning in fact do. But everybody meanwhile does not want to reflect on this, but rather wants to ensure that institutions of learning will teach skills instead of facts. Facts, say the skills-people, change with the growth of knowledge. And since the higher learning is nothing if not education for a lifetime, it certainly does not want to be sued by Mary Lou Smith—believe me it doesn't!—when she turns forty and finds that some of the true facts she learned in chemistry or sociology have now become false facts. Therefore, say the skills-people, it is the main job of liberal learning to teach skills, because if people acquire the right skills then they can get all the facts they want whenever they want them, besides which they can solve problems! And to get a good job in the problem-solving society, one must be able to solve problems. So the aim of a college education should be to teach people problem-solving skills.

The eschatologist, who, you will remember, did not want to be a fact, has an even greater aversion to being a problem and a paralyzing fear of becoming a solution. His thoughts return anon to the logician in *Rhinoceros* who, in the process of teaching people how to solve the rhinoceros-problem, became a pachyderm himself, for which a bowler hat does not entirely compensate.

Now eschatologists are not known as teetotalers. And this one thinks that solving a problem is O.K. now and then, or rather that it would be O.K. if it could be done in moderation. The trouble is, however, that few people have the willpower to resist solving a second problem after they have solved the first, the second usually being caused by the solution to the first. By the time people are on their fourth or fifth problem, they are irrevocably hooked, hard-core addicts, who will then do anything—absolutely anything—for a fix. Do not be deceived by the cocker spaniel friendliness of the addicted problem solver. Look rather at his glazed eyes. He would solve his own mother without a second thought if she became a problem.

Problem-solvers often have no intentions beyond solving whatever problem may happen to present itself. But almost as often they have the very best of intentions indeed, a circumstance which, however, does little to alter the reality that, in their encounter with problem-solving, living creatures usually lose.

Consider the case of the California condors. Those magnificent birds are dying out, the victims of the accumulated previous solutions to industrial and economic problems. But the problem-solving society cares, so it has taken to heart the plight of the giant birds. A team of naturalists from the Audubon society is trying to solve the condor problem. But solving a problem depends on figuring out what it is. One must have reliable information about what exactly is killing the condors. To find that out, one must naturally make close scientific observations of the condors. And so the dedicated naturalists climb the jagged cliffs of the California coast up to the roosts of the condors, where they capture them and tranquilize them, and take blood samples, and tag them, and implant radio transmitters in them. This permits their problematic condition to be analyzed in the fullest scientific detail.

These ministrations, on which the very solution to the condor-problem depends, have an unfortunate effect on the condors. The great birds have difficulty adjusting to being problems, and so, when subjected to all this beneficent technological solicitude, they tend to die of maladjustment. It is bad enough, reasons the condor, to be the victim of the pollution of the human industrial problem-solving machine. But to be made over into a problem in addition—well, that is simply too much for any self-respecting condor to accept, and so, when the problem-solver lays hands on him, he quivers with every feather of his being, and, obeying the wisdom of instinct, expires on the spot.

Pondering this example, an eschatologist is inclined to wonder whether the minds of students tend to expire under all the solicitude of the great higher problem-solving machine. Something must be causing the current deadness.

For those who are not moved by the heroic self-sacrifice of the condors, perhaps the fate of the innocent tomato may serve as an eschatological warning.

Some years ago at a large and famous university, agricultural engineers developed a tomato harvester to solve the problem of how to pick three acres of tomatoes an hour. But their gleaming new invention turned out to have a problem. Not only did it pick tomatoes at the rate of three acres an hour, it also squashed them to a pulp at the rate of three acres an hour.

Now in the rational world that many people think they live in, the tomato-picker would be written off as a bad solution, a failure, so to speak; and the agri-engineers would have to go back to the drawing board. But in the actual world of problem-solving that eschatologists know they live in, it was much easier to redesign the tomato than to scrap years of reseach and government support that had been invested in building the machine. So the problem-solvers of the higher agri-school set out to remake the disgustingly inefficient tomato which could not adapt to the demands of modern life.

Eventually they bred a tomato with a skin so tough that one could drop it on a concrete floor from a height of five feet and it would not break open. (Indeed, it had twice the impact resistance pound for pound than the government's safety standards for car bumpers require!)

The new species was called the MH-1. Needless to say, the tomato harvester could not squash the MH-1 at the rate of three acres an hour. It could not even dent it at the rate of three acres an hour.

And so mankind progressed by solving the tomato problem.

But it is the way of solutions to beget new problems. For one thing, the MH-1 would not turn red on the vine. Even when it was fully ripe it had an eerie greenish color. For another, it lacked essential vitamins and food value. And for still another, it did not taste like a tomato, nor, for that matter, like anything else ever grown in the rich soil of the earth.

But agri-men are nothing if not determined. And these minor problems were not to elude solution. They devised a machine to turn the MH-1 red, so that even if it did not glisten red on the vine, it would glisten red in the supermarket. Next they designed a machine to inject vitamins and nutrients into the new improved tomato as it rolled down the conveyor to be packed. Finally, the problem of taste is not much of a problem in an essentially tasteless society. The packers, shippers, and retailers were delighted to have the new toughskin tomato, because it vastly reduced losses in shipping. That left only the customers. And they soon forgot about the old antiquated tomatoes that glistened red on the vine, as they bought the new improved model that glistened red in the supermarket. They were helped to adjust to this progress perhaps by the fact that there was soon no other kind of tomatoes to buy.

Now to this very day when you go to the Piggly Wiggly, you will not find tomatoes there, but solutions costing 79¢ a pound. Yet, as you have probably already guessed, even the best of solutions is not without its problems. The MH-1 has a tragic flaw. It resembles its hapless ancestor in being round. Unfortunately for it, however, the packages in which it is packed are rectangular. Round tomatoes waste space in oblong packages. So back at the old drawing board, the lights burn late in the agri-lab, while the best agri-minds in the agri-business are striving to solve X for the following equation: $(MH-1) + X = (MH-1)^2$.

Who then among you would bet a bushel of tomatoes—you know,

the old fashioned kind that glisten red on the vine when you are out in the patch on a bright July morning with a salt shaker in your hand, letting the juice of life dribble down your chin—who then, I ask, would bet a bushel of such tomatoes that the new problem of squaring the circle in tomato-research will not soon be solved?

Certainly not an eschatologist.

As the eschatological parable of the tomato teaches, South of Eden human beings adapt the human ends they seek to fit the means they have available to realize them. Thus problem-solving does not require in practice what it seems to require in theory, that a solution ultimately satisfy criteria that are given in the definition of the problem. Rather, it permits any solution, that happens for one reason or another to establish itself, to redefine the nature of the original problem. Thus the human purposes that impelled the search for a solution in the first place are redefined to fit the solution.

This is what it means to live in a progressive society. If a tomato that we wish to pick more efficiently turns out to be maladapted to the efficient solution we devise for picking it, it is necessary to redesign the tomato. If the grading system that institutions of learning have devised to measure, uniformly and efficiently, the learning of the students then comes to supplant that learning, so that students become uniformly more interested in the grade than in learning, and come to equate learning with earning a grade, do colleges and universities redesign the means which now defeat the original end? By no means. Rather it becomes necessary to accommodate subject matter, teaching methods, and testing to the students' paramount interest in the grade. The higher learning is then content to graduate the human equivalent of the MH-1, which will never be bruised by learning.

Thus eschatology leads to the conclusion that the means-ends reversal implicit in the peculiar ideology of problem-solving is *the* problem, and that solutions are not the solution.

Nevertheless, condors or no condors, tomatoes or no tomatoes, learning or no learning, eschatology or no eschatology, problem-solving is here to stay. For acquiring problem-solving skills in some area is not only the path to a satisfying career, but puts one in touch with the real world. This is because problem-solving is the true metaphysics of modern life, and so shapes the prevailing sense of reality. In the metaphysical vision of the problem-solving society nothing is real unless it has a solution, that is, unless it presents itself as a problem.

In the metaphysics of problem-solving there are two kinds of problems: those that have been solved, and those that have not been solved—yet. The vast aggregate of already solved problems determines the possibilities for defining any new problem. It must be conceived in such a way that the range of its possible solutions shows the minimum conflict possible with the totality of already existing solutions.

There is no such thing as a solutionless problem. For, in order for something to be a problem, it must by definition have a solution, even if we have not discovered what it is or may never discover what it is. A solutionless problem, therefore, fails to register on the problem-solving mentality. To speak of it is like pressing the shutter with no film in the camera. As a consequence there is no mystery, nothing unresolvable in the universe of the problem-solver. For he will either turn the mysterious into a problem, in which case it is no longer mysterious, or he will simply be unable to acknowledge its existence. Thus everything, absolutely everything, that seeks the dignity of reality in the problem-solving society must first renounce its citizenship in any other realm of Being and be naturalized as a problem.

The inability to set any limits on the area to which problem-solving might apply is the definitive characteristic of the modern technical order. It has made all things human into technological problems. Raising children has become a problem. One needs books, consultations with experts, and support groups, before one can suckle one's young or paddle them. One's sex life (no one had a sex life before the rise of the problem-solving order, which does not mean, of course, that there was an absence of sex) is a problem. The latest techniques must be applied to its solution. One's marriage is a problem. One must see a marriage counselor. One's morale on the job is a problem. The management must solve the problem, a task rather like spraying insecticide on a row of cabbages that is infested with beetles. One's image is a problem. One must hire a public relations consultant to solve it.

And the natural, inevitable outcome of all this, is that people have become problems. Adolf Eichmann was perhaps the most famous pioneer in the search for "solutions" in this area. Who was this man, really? The devil incarnate? The face of unspeakable evil? He was an affable, rather ordinary problem-solver, signing forms in triplicate in his office which would solve the Jewish problem, and then exchanging pleasantries with his co-workers in adjoining offices.

His "final solution" turned people into lampshades at Auschwitz. Problem-solving has since become more humane. In its more enlightened forms, it only burns out people's bulbs by getting them to view themselves as problems. Since they are then eager to solve themselves, government intervention is no longer needed.

I once met a behaviorist psychologist who was trying to give up smoking. She saw her smoking behavior as the essence of the problem. And she attempted to solve it, with the same technical proficiency that she used in controlling the various wanted and unwanted behaviors of rats, by rigging up a cigarette pack so that it would deliver intermittent electric shocks when she reached for a smoke. The issue is not whether this works (I never found out), nor even that there are not certain conditions under which such a technique might be resorted to, but rather that it never even occurred to her to think of herself as an agent with a human will, who might *choose* to resist her habit, even if in the end she should fail most miserably. It is, in any case, far better to succumb to smoke, than to perceive one's life as a series of behaviors to be controlled, that is, as a sequence of problems to be solved. The behaviorist, of course, was only trying to be real in the only way the contemporary ontology permits people to be real. She was only trying to solve herself.

Eschatology has never been popular with the problem-solvers. They will tend to regard the foregoing reflections as deranged, or, what amounts to the same thing, as pessimistic. But an eschatologist is not without his own brand of hope. He finds it in the great example of Job:

> Now there was a day when the sons of God came to present themselves before the Lord, and Satan also came among them.
>
> The Lord said to Satan: "Whence have you come?"
>
> Satan answered the Lord: "I've been jogging down on earth and checking the place out."
>
> And the Lord said to Satan: "Have you checked out my man, Job, that there is none like him on the earth, a blameless and upright cat, who fears God and turns away from problem-solving?"
>
> Then Satan answered the Lord: "Hells bells! Does Job fear God for nothing, man? Hast Thou not put a plastic dome over his house and all that he hath, and given the sucker a free ride so that he hath no prob-

lems? But sign this waiver and let me mess him over a bit and surround him with problems, and I'll lay Thee twenty at ten to one, that he'll try to solve them to Thy face."

Then the Lord said to Satan: "You're on. Behold all that he has is in your power, and you may heap problems upon him like a garbage truck unloading at the city dump, only don't mess with his head."

So Satan went down to the college where Job taught, and said: "Behold I shall cause Job's students to die in their fields, and they shall sit vacantly in rows in front of him, and having eyes they shall see not, and having ears they shall hear not. Then Job will regard them as problems and attempt to solve them, or my name ain't Lucifer."

And Satan said, further, "Behold I will cause the faculty to die in their fields, and their wise men to babble like idiots in their assemblies, and dark counsel to be mistaken for light. Then they will vote all manner of solutions to their problems. And Job won't have a Chinaman's chance in hell of avoiding all this faculty problem-solving. He'll even be thinking up solutions himself, or yours truly ain't the Prince of Darkness."

"And behold," quoth Satan, being somewhat long-winded, "I will cause the administration to start devising solutions—yea, even to problems that no one has thought up yet. And the solutions will be as waves of the sea as they dash against the rocks, and each new solution will break apart into twelve new problems even as there are twelve tribes in Israel. And, if I'm any judge of man-flesh, Job will cop out on the whole godless scene and jump into problem-solving so fast that he'll look like A. J. Foyt at the Indy 500, or my name ain't Beelzebub."

And Satan did unto Job just like he said he would. And when Job saw what was coming down, he said: "Naked I came from my mother's womb, and naked I shall return; the Lord gave, and the Lord has taken away, blessed be the name of the Lord."

And in all this Job did not lift a finger to solve a single problem. The thought never even crossed his mind.

And the Lord said to Satan: "Where's my two hundred? Check out my man, Job. There is none like him on the earth, a blameless and upright cat, who still fears God and turns away from solutions. He has still got it together, even though you got me to let you mess with him and load him down with problems."

And Satan, who was basically a welsher and mean as a cottonmouth besides, said: "Skin for skin! (which means in Hebrew exactly what you think it means). All that a man has he will give to keep from cracking up. Thou wast loath to let me mess with his head before, but now sign this, and let me screw with his mind. I'll blow the top of his head so high it will make Mt. St. Helens look like a flicked Bic. And there won't be no kind of solution that he won't try then, or my name ain't Moloch."

And the Lord said to Satan: "O.K., but don't kill him."

So Satan went down and got on Job's case and afflicted him with severe alienation—so that Job was paralyzed from the neck up and could no longer think straight, or teach good, or write clear. His greatest ambition in life then was to stay in bed in the morning.

So Job sat at home watching "Dallas" on TV and drinking two six-packs a night.

Then his wife said to him: "Are you still on your integrity kick? For God's sake, do something! I can't take it any more! Get off your behind and find a solution. Curse the Dean and let's get the hell out of this crummy place. You can probably get a job with an insurance company or at least on a newspaper somewhere, and I'll go to law school."

But he rebuked her sharply, saying: "Knock it off woman! What do you want me to do, for Godsake? Dabble in solutions? Shall we receive good at the hands of God and not receive problems?"

And in all this Job did not really sin with his lips, even though he did use the word "solution" once.

You know the rest of the story. How Job's comforters came and found him sitting alone in the faculty lounge and told him that his condition was plainly due to his failure to deal with his problems. How they then proposed various solutions like assertiveness training, and transactional analysis, and EST, and biofeedback, and told him to read *Passages* and that he was having a mid-life crisis, which was normal enough if he'd just admit it and get in touch with his feelings. How in general they tried to get him to agree that *he*, Job of Uz, was the problem, and that the first step to any solution was to admit he was a problem. How Job then screamed a truly primal scream and refused to admit that he was a problem! How he then told his so-called friends to cram their silly solutions. How he didn't want to talk to them anyhow, but to God to find out why things had gotten so heavy all of a sudden, and in particular why the Lord was trying to get him to solve himself.

How he finally got to talk to the Lord, and the Lord did most of the talking. How the Lord showed him a rhinoceros (called Behemoth in those days) and explained to him that unless he could make one, he had better just shut up, and that if other folks wanted to try to make one or be one then that was *their* problem. How the Lord then told Job to stop whining and griping.

How Job then repented "in dust and ashes." How his "friends" were then punished for telling him that he was a problem for which there was bound to be a solution.

And how the Lord then vindicated Job because he had refused to solve problems and become one himself; and how the Lord then saw to it that Job never had to think about problems again, and how Job then lived a long happy life and died at the age of a hundred and forty, being old and "full of days."

We have it, then, on good authority that solutions never solve anything. That is not to say, of course, that we have no serious problems.

Interlude: Call Al-Anon

In the land of problem-solving, due West of Uz and South of Eden, no one becomes an eschatologist without first walking through the Valley of the Shadow of Reform. The only shade in the Valley is under the Tree of the Consciousness of Possible Improvements. The Valley is a hard place and it teaches hard lessons. The hardest lesson it teaches is that institutions of the highest learning, as well as institutions of the lowest learning, as well as institutions of the most middling learning, flatly refuse to reform. This is mostly because they don't want to. But it is also because they can't. It doesn't make a lot of difference whether they can't because they don't want to, or don't want to because they can't. In any event they won't.

Everybody agrees, of course, when they think about it, that institutions need to reform. Even an institution often agrees with that, and it often sincerely promises to—with the sincerity of Jack Lemmon in *Days of Wine and Roses*. The institution is beguilingly sincere at that moment and it tugs at the heartstrings of the reformer and pleads to be trusted. But then when the reformer isn't looking, the institution rationalizes to itself that it, after all, should hardly be expected to reform, unless the sorry and hostile and generally pusillanimous world out there that is responsible for its present depravity reforms; and so it decides that it doesn't have to unless and until all the other no good institutions reform.

And then the institution, feeling infinitely self-justified, sneaks out the bottle of Wild Turkey that it has hidden under its Procrustean bed and is off on another bender again. So the reformer comes and finds it sprawled in some back alley, burping and belching, and puking and farting, and generally degrading itself. When it sobers up, it will, of course, sincerely repent, promise never, never, to do it again, and plead for another chance, a plea to which the softhearted reformer is going to yield again, or else he would not be a reformer. Then the institution will promptly go off on another drunk again at the next opportunity.

When the reformer finally wises up he will know a hard eschatological truth: institutions cannot reform, they can only change in accordance with a law of cosmic dissipation that states: *plus ça change c'est plus la même chose.*

Up Against the Wall, Metathinker!

Universities are a legacy of the Middle Ages. In those days in those places learning had a focal point. Theology was queen of the sciences. And theologians could become absorbed in the question: how many angels can dance on the head of a pin? This question is now ridiculed as the very paradigm of a decadent scholasticism in an advanced world of learning where mathematical sociologists write dissertations on

"Group Formations on the Johns Hopkins Quadrangle on Sunday Afternoons," where behaviorists prove by schedules of reinforcement that children tend to smile more when given candy, where philosophers write about "Three Ways of Spilling Ink," and where animal psychologists, the true missionaries of all this learning, try to teach language to the great apes. Yet the question was of strategic importance to medieval thought, which conceived reality as a hierarchy of substances, a view which worked fine for ordinary substances like rocks and trees and even people, and for the extraordinary substance, God, but got into trouble with the intermediate case of angels, who, being many, displayed some of the traits of ordinary substances and who, being immaterial, displayed one of the traits of God. In their much ridiculed question, the medieval schoolmen were only trying to come to grips with the mystery of immaterial substance.

The enigma of immaterial substance has by no means vanished as a challenge for the modern university, where management now reigns as the queen of the sciences and learning has no focus. But it has been largely suppressed by the modern schoolmen. One of the chief aims of eschatological reflection is to restore the question of immaterial substance to its rightful place as the key to the modern organization of knowledge. Of course, the question can no longer be about angels since there do not seem to be any, a matter presumably established by the etymological consideration that *angelos* means "messenger" in Greek and no messages are getting through to the modern university.

Since a modern formulation, accordingly, cannot be about angels dancing on pinheads, an eschatologically more promising approach may be to begin with the pinheads themselves and ask: how many workshops on workshops can a pinhead attend before he comes to realize that he is an immaterial substance? And this immediately suggests a further question: how many workshops on workshops can be held before it will occur to some pinhead to hold a workshop on workshops on workshops? These are troublesome questions. It is not easy to do full eschatological justice to the question of immaterial substance today. But we will try our best.

It is generally agreed by those who have thought about it that the mystery of immaterial substance in the modern world is inextricably linked to the great cultural metamorphosis — the age ushered in by the rise of the metapeople. They appeared in great numbers just about the time the higher learning found itself saddled with problems, and so became a problem-solving institution.

The metapeople, the immaterial substances of the contemporary academic world, disseminate meta-activity and metathinking through all academic fields, as well as throughout the para-academic pursuits that have become so absolutely essential in a well-run, efficiently managed college or university.

In the strictly academic areas, their trademark is a language that never touches Mother Earth. Given the importance of skills in contemporary higher education, it is appropriate to take an example of metawriting from an eminent social scientist who appears to be discussing them:

> Skills constitute the manipulative techniques of human goal attainment and control in relation to the physical world, so far as artifacts or machines especially designed as tools do not yet supplement them. Truly human skills are guided by organized and codified knowledge of both the things to be manipulated and the human capacities that are used to manipulate them. Such knowledge is an aspect of cultural-level symbolic processes, and, like other aspects to be discussed presently, requires the capacities of the human central nervous system, particularly the brain. This organic system is clearly essential to all of the symbolical processes; as we well know, the human brain is far superior to the brain of any other species.[3]

In eschatological translation,this appears to mean that knowing how to do something, like, say, writing an intelligible English paragraph, requires a developed brain. Metawriters are continually fascinated by the existence of the human brain, and tend to dwell on it inordinately.

There are cynical theorists — Stanislav Andreski, for one — who explain the phenomenon of metaspeech as a coverup for rather sleazy human motives: ". . . if you reiterate the same few notions in a language which (though open to serious criticism) is at least comprehensible, people will eventually notice the repetition, whereas if you wrap them up in incomprehensible mumbo-jumbo, you can go on and on safely

---

[3]Talcott Parsons, *Societies: Evolutionary and Comparative Perspectives,* quoted in Stanislav Andreski, *Social Science as Sorcery* (New York: St. Martin's Press, 1973), p. 60.

without anybody knowing what you are saying anyway."[4] People, he thinks, use metawriting to further their scholarly ambitions while concealing their intellectual limitations.

But eschatology rejects this explanation on the grounds that meta-people are not people at all, but, as the Greek prefix meaning "after" implies, a race that came *after* people. The after-people simply have no motives of any kind, nor are they capable of grasping the customs and motives of the ancient race of earth dwellers, whom they so largely displaced in the higher learning, probably because these customs were based to some extent on their fascinating brains. One should never impute human motivations, however shabby, to metapersons.

The metapeople are also ubiquitous in the para-academic arrangements of the new higher learning, although it is increasingly hard to draw the line between the academic and the para-academic in a metainstitution. Today all good colleges and universities bustle with meta-activity. It may consist in getting grants, or getting grants for getting grants, planning conferences on planning to plan, sponsoring seminars on teaching and learning (which are now intransitive meta-verbs), holding conferences on all manner of skills, giving seminars in problem-solving, seeking input and feedback, and, of course, conducting periodic workshops on workshops. The para-academic metapeople generally metathink of themselves as "facilitators." Indeed when no other clue is available they can always be recognized as metapeople by their propensity to use the word "facilitate" at the slightest provocation, and often without the slightest provocation. They also prioritize in the course of facilitating.

The facilitators are, as it were, the enzymes that play such a crucial role in the metabolic processes of the higher metalearning as it tries to digest everything. Though the modern metauniversity's compulsive desire to eat the universe is not yet fully understood, Christopher Lasch, a formidable eschatologist in his own right, has given the best account we have of it to date. He points out that it is increasingly taken for granted that "higher learning ideally includes everything, assimilates all of life." School then becomes a total institution, and nothing escapes "educationalization."

The university has boiled all experience down into "courses" of study—a culinary image appropriate to

---

[4]Stanislav Andreski, *Social Science as Sorcery*, p. 57.

the underlying ideal of enlightened consumption. In its eagerness to embrace experience, the university comes to serve as a substitute for it. In doing so, however, it merely compounds its intellectual failures— notwithstanding its claim to prepare students for "life." Not only does higher education destroy the students' minds; it incapacitates them emotionally as well, rendering them incapable of confronting experience without benefit of textbooks, grades, and pre-digested points of view. Far from preparing students to live "authentically," the higher learning in America leaves them unable to perform the simplest task—to prepare a meal or go to a party or get into bed with a member of the opposite sex—without elaborate academic instruction. The only thing it leaves to chance is higher learning.[5]

Whatever the causes of the meta-appetite that Lasch describes, it clearly reflects the institutionalization of metathinking. It is, at the most general level, just the tendency to substitute the means, the methods, and arrangements of the educational process, for the end, the original concrete activity for which the means were originally devised. Wherever this means-ends reversal is found, there you will also find a mob of metapeople busily planning seminars on growth and seeking other ways to prepare people for life.

The origin of the metapeople is a matter of some controversy. Some say they are fallen angels, who fell with Lucifer, the most substantial immaterial substance, or at least joined him about the time he decided to pester Job. It is said that having fallen, they simply bided their time until the higher learning offered them the chance to wrap their immaterial selves in the regalia of academic respectability. But this account is probably and old wives' tale.

Others suggest that they stem from an ancient race of academics, who in the twilight of the old academy were forced to attend too many committee meetings. It is well known that committees are lethal in the root sense of forcing those who must sit through them to drink deep draughts of the waters of *Lethe*. Thus, as this view would have it, when

---

[5]Lasch, *Narcissism*, p. 153.

they had drunk their fill, they were ferried across the Styx to become academic shades. The proponents of this view make much of the meaning of the Greek prefix and contend that this proves that meta-activity is the substance of the afterlife. The theory goes on to claim that these shades did not much care for their shadiness, and so in a violation of the cosmic arrangements worthy of the genius of Sophocles, they pretended to be real, persuaded themselves that they were, and left the netherworld for jobs in the metaworld just about the time of the great knowledge explosion. This might have been a harmless, if somewhat shady prank, were it not for the circumstance that Queen Management is no respecter of persons and cannot distinguish a shade from a mortal. This theory has its ardent defenders, of course, but there are those who think it is pure myth.

A more modern variant of this theory has it that the metapeople are vampires, the living dead, who must suck the blood of real substance in order to sustain their illusory metaexistences. But though this theory has some empirical merit, it succumbs to the difficulty that, unlike vampires, the metapeople are not afraid to expose themselves in full daylight.

Eschatologists have no desire to contribute to the survival of superstitions. They wish at all costs to avoid even the appearance of doing so. Thus we must leave these speculations and confine the rest of this account to what can be known with certainty.

The pedestrian truth of the matter is this.

About fifty years ago, the prefix "meta" began to appear in philosophical jargon as a way of generating and defining new branches of inquiry. Logic spawned metalogic, mathematics gave rise to metamathematics, and ethics engendered metaethics. To take the last case, a person who occupies himself with ethics tries to determine the nature of good and evil and how to live so as to espouse the former and eschew the latter. Whatever the answers, the questions are real human questions that pertain to living real human lives in a concrete world. Metaethics is another matter. It does not aim to arrive at conclusions about good and evil and how to live, but to arrive at a *description* of what people are doing when they try to arrive at conclusions about good and evil and how to live. Thus its task is not to engage in ethical thinking at all, but to *describe* ethical thinking. Its purpose, in short, is not to think but to metathink, which is to *think about thinking* about something.

In itself metaethics might have been relatively innocuous. It might even have turned up a useful insight here and there. But it immodestly refused to remain in itself. Instead, its practitioners acted as if the new enterprise completely superseded the old human ethics on which it depended. It became the common wisdom that one had to think metaethically before one could think ethically, which completely reversed the reasoning that had brought metaethics into being in the first place. And since the new discipline was so fascinating and had so many unexplored areas, as new fields always do, one could spend a professional lifetime just metathinking about ethics and never discover a "window" for reentry into the earth's atmosphere. Thus the orbiting metaethicist forgot about the moral life on earth. Preferring weightlessness, he substituted the encapsulated life of description and method and analysis for the earthbound life of mortals with its gravity of choice and risk. These first metaspace pioneers thus developed no very profound views of good and evil, except of course that it was good when the learned journals accepted their articles and evil when they did not. On the other hand, they amassed a vast technical knowledge about the words "good" and "evil" and about what other people had said in their efforts to find out how to live, and how they had said it, and about whether they had said it clearly or ambiguously.

The new philosophical attitude quickly pushed out beyond the confines of metaethics to claim the very soul of the philosopher in all his professional endeavors. G. E. Moore, perhaps the most meta of all metathinkers who ever set pen to paper, says in his *Autobiography:*

> I do not think that the world or the sciences would ever have suggested to me any philosophic problems. What has suggested philosophical problems to me is things which other philosophers have said about the world or the sciences.[6]

This metarevelation should be read in the light of a comment by Schopenhauer, one of the best eschatologists of the nineteenth century. He wrote:

> A man becomes a philosopher by reason of a certain perplexity from which he seeks to free himself. . . .

---

[6]G. E. Moore, "Autobiography" in *The Philosophy of G. E. Moore*, ed. Paul Schilpp (New York: Tudor, 1942), p. 14.

But what distinguishes the false philosopher from the true is this: the perplexity of the latter arises from the contemplation of the world itself, while that of the former results from some book, some system of philosophy which lies before him.[7]

It is unnecessary to subscribe to the dubious thesis that philosophical ideas, or even just plain ideas, have had a significant impact on the recent course of the higher learning to agree that the metamorphosis within philosophy is a paradigm for the transformation of the entire academy into a metaculture. The powerful engine of metathought not only propelled the philosophers away from the world of experience but professionals in all other academic fields and the para-academic enterprises as well. This is in accordance with the fundamental eschatological law that, other things being equal, metathinking will metastasize indefinitely. Needless to say, in the modern university other things are always equal.

Whenever there is an ongoing inquiry about something of concrete importance here on earth, it is also possible to metathink about that inquiry. And given enough metathinking, any sense of what is concretely important will vanish. For the original concrete issue then recedes from view, as the act of inquiring, and the method of inquiring, and the logic of inquiring, and the psychological motives for inquiring, are abstracted from it.

These abstractions are metathoughts. But the abstract metathoughts are immediately reconcretized. First, because even the most gaseous of abstractions have a general tendency to crystalize in the mind. Second, because anything becomes real in the world if enough people are willing to talk about it. And third, because in the modern university, which has no compass to steer by, one landfall is as good as another. Thus metathoughts have no difficulty institutionalizing themselves in metadisciplines. This happens as follows. The congealed metathoughts become a self-contained body of knowledge in the minds of a few pioneers. Then they acquire ontological standing by being mentioned in the education section of *Newsweek*. Soon the metasooners rush into the territory opened up by the early settlers and the metabody of knowledge becomes a discipline with practitioners. Next

[7]Arthur Schopenhauer, *The World as Will and Idea*, trans. R. B. Haldane and J. Kemp, 3 volumes (London: Routledge and Kegan Paul, 1883), 1:41.

the metabody is housed in an academic department, the most concrete of all academic concrescences, and acquires all the rights and privileges appertaining to any legitimate body of knowledge. Then it is taught by the great higher teaching machine to a generation of unsuspecting students. They have no way of knowing that all they are getting is metaknowledge, having been in school so long that they have no feel for reality. Besides there is no one to tell them. The philosophers, whose job it used to be to spot this sort of thing, are all too busy writing the metamanual for the new field. In a short while, tens of thousands of metatrainees march across the stage like little toy soldiers to receive their diplomas and be metacertified.

After several academic generations of this, there come to be vastly more metapeople in the higher learning than ordinary earth dwellers. And the metapeople expect to be accorded all the perquisites of their high calling in the meta-academy as they pass along their metaexperience to others, even though all they unknowingly know has application only within the complex of the institutional metaexperience that metathinking created in the first place.

The latest entry in the metafield is a journal called *Metamedicine*. No doubt it aims to help physicians stay abreast of the latest methods of treating the metaly ill.

So the metainstitution is erected on the ruins of the old human learning, which in turn becomes a fading memory.

Franz Kafka, that sly old eschatologist who knew about metamorphoses, also understood the mechanics of the current transformation. His parable, "Leopards in the Temple," states:

> Leopards break into the temple and drink to the dregs what is in the sacrificial pitchers; this is repeated over and over again; finally it can be calculated in advance, and it becomes a part of the ceremony.[8]

Nowhere are the facilitations and metafacilitations of the metamind more apparent than in its efforts to solve the problem of teaching and learning in colleges and universities during the last two decades. In fact, the very existence of the problem of teaching and learning in the last two decades may be the crowning achievement of the metamentality.

---

[8]Franz Kafka, *Parables and Paradoxes* (New York: Schocken Press, 1946), p. 93.

Before the invasion of the metathinkers, teaching and learning were rarely discussed much in colleges and universities. It was taken for granted that if real professors were occupied with things that mattered to them in the presence of real students, they would then be engaged in teaching and the students would then tend to learn (not all equally, of course, but that was the best people could do South of Eden). It was thought sufficient for an educational institution to provide a place and a regular time for the students to get together with the professor for learning and teaching to occur, and no one bothered to give it a metathought. Some professors, of course, would be liked; others would not. Some would lecture; and some would just talk or even listen in their classes. Some would be boring; others exciting. Some would fancy themselves indispensable to the students' understanding of their subject; others would act more as mediators between the student and the discipline. Some would care deeply about the personal lives of their students and the relation of their subjects to them; others would not. And, naturally enough, in this very human world, some of the professors would do their jobs well; while others would do them badly. And some students would not learn even when it was done well; while others would learn even when it was done very badly. That was all there was to it. It was far from a perfect situation; but then South of Eden things never are perfect. It was nevertheless vastly better than what was to follow.

For the old human learning did not really have any general concept answering to the terms "teaching" and "learning," because their meaning was understood to shift from discipline to discipline in important ways, and, of course, from individual to individual. In short, the old human learning had simply not abstracted from the obvious and natural activity in which it was engaged, and so had not metathought about it. This circumstance left people free to think about other things—their intellectual interests, for instance—and to share them with the students.

Then one cloudless September morning comes a metaexpert to the old academy, and with his unerring instinct to abstract the heart from any matter, formally announces that since teaching and learning, as he has noticed, are the universal activities of educational institutions, they must be urgently metathought about, lest they be carried on inefficiently and inadequately and badly. Indeed, he declares, they can be much improved by incorporating the findings of the latest metaresearch into teaching methods, teaching strategies, and feedback procedures. Who would then dare to raise his voice against progress and new findings, especially in an institution of learning?

So the Copernican Revolution begins. Teaching and learning, abstracted from their organic and individual setting, are recrystallized as metaconcepts applicable to every "learning environment" or "teaching situation." Thus the new metanotion comes to denote an abstract relation, and the old human educators who were engaged in a concrete practice become the *relata* of the metarelation, mere instances of the hypostatized relation: X teaches Y to Z, Z learns Y from X. Who X is does not matter. Who Z is does not matter. What Y is does not matter. X, Y, and Z stand for the interchangeable parts of the teaching machine designed to produce a product called learning. And the machine can be made more efficient. Efficiency is the sole measure of the worth of a machine.

So it is not surprising that the cogs in the machine will soon begin to cogitate. Then they will begin to have metacognitions about what they are doing in their classrooms. These cognitions in turn will leave less time to devote to the original activity which they are intended to promote. Worse, they will make the cogs vastly more self-conscious about the time they do spend in the original activity.

Once a certain level of self-consciousness has been attained, the cogs will want to know whether they are doing well or badly by metastandards. Or if they have managed to keep their wits, and prefer not to know, the administration will certainly want to know.

Then the metaexpert will come to their aid with a standardized evaluation instrument that can quantify good and evil teaching, giving one an *objective* yardstick to measure one's performance. The new measuring instrument will measure the mean number of students in a given class who were "turned on" by the Magna Carta, or Plato's Cave, or quadratic equations, or by Ozymandias who said, "Look on my works, ye Mighty, and despair!" And teaching and learning can now be measurably improved by improving the mean number of students who liked a given course, expressed as a percentile of the mean number of students in a national population who developed a mean liking for learning in the various courses they took, which may or may not have been about the Magna Carta, or Plato's Cave, or quadratic equations, or Ozymandias, who said, "Look on my works, ye Mighty, and despair!," and which may or may not have been taught by professors who themselves once had a mean liking for students and their disciplines and their professions but, without quite knowing why, have been developing a mean apathy or a mean meanness.

Bemused by the rise of TEACHING AND LEARNING, the eschatologist keeps hearing the haunting opening lines of a poem he once knew by Christian Morgenstern, which is about a solitary knee on a journey through the cosmos:

> *Ein Knie geht einsam durch die Welt,*
> *Es ist ein Knie sonst nichts.*

And he muses further that the metanotions of teaching and learning are rather like that knee, a veritable metaknee, divorced from its organic setting as part of an individual, wandering aimlessly in the void.

And, then, entranced by that knee, he suddenly sees where it is all leading: If the metapeople have their way we will soon live in a world where everyone who teaches anything will first have to be taught to teach before he can teach. And everyone who wants to learn anything will first have to learn to learn before he can learn. And as it escapes the gravitational pull of the earth and heads into deep metaspace, meta-thinking will encounter no further resistance. It will at that point extend to limits of the universe and curve back on itself, and be applied with an inevitable metalogic to itself. For obviously if you are going to teach someone to teach, you are going to need a teacher to teach him to teach. And it is unmetathinkable that the teacher of such an essential subject should himself be unmetatrained in it. Ergo, we cannot but assent to the metametaconclusion that we shall have to teach teachers to teach to teach. And these teachers will in turn need teachers—*ad infinitum.* Here is the fulfillment of the great American dream, a growth industry with a truly infinite capacity for expansion, to gladden the heart of even the most bearish Wall Street analyst.

Meanwhile as the metamarket booms, the few remaining souls who did not get in on the ground floor, have no choice but to pursue eschatology. It is said that there is something distinctly medieval about this dwindling breed, and it is rumored, though we cannot vouch for it here, that they keep fully stocked pin cushions strewn about in their offices in the hope of attracting a passing flock of angels back to their favorite haunt. Some say they hope by this stratagem to receive a message that will finally clear up the mystery of immaterial substance. But that too is only a rumor.

Last Thoughts about the Last Things

It is time to bring these reflections to a close. They cannot have an ending, of course. But they can be stopped. In stopping, the eschatologist wishes to address some of the myths and misunderstandings that surround his craft.

It is, for example, sometimes alleged by the enemies of eschatology that those who pursue the practice are Luddites or romantics who languish in a long forgotten past and would like nothing better than to turn the clock back. Eschatologists, for their part, do not see any point in moving the hands of a stopped clock in any direction. Certainly, they have no desire whatever to emulate Miniver Cheevy, who, "born too late," then "wept that he was ever born, for he had reasons." Eschatologists do not often weep no matter what the reason. Mostly they're glad to be survivors, and even happier to know that they are. They are not ashamed to enjoy all the blessings of modern life. They sometimes eat at McDonald's, visit their dentists twice a year, complain about their high taxes, and have dishwashers in their suburban homes. (Most draw the line at golf, however.) They certainly do not advocate renouncing all these blessings. But they do believe that people may have paid a far higher price than they dream for these modern comforts, and they suspect the prevailing attitude toward them has had something to do with why their clocks have stopped. But despite this aberration, eschatologists are by and large nice people who will not embarrass anyone who invites them to a backyard barbecue.

More serious is the charge that eschatology is just a cover for cynicism. This too is calumny. Cynicism, historically considered, is the view that nothing exists, but that if anything should nevertheless happen to exist, it would not be any good anyway. Eschatologists think, on the contrary, that there have been some good things in the world and that there still are some. Indeed their main contention is that the higher learning has forgotten what they are.

Before disappearing into Mexico, Ambrose Bierce wrote an epitaph that may serve as a warning to cynics:

Cynic, perforce, from study of mankind
In the false volume of his single mind
He damned his fellows for his own unworth
And, bad himself, thought nothing good on earth
He yearned to squander what he lived to save
And did not, for he could not, cheat the grave.

No self-respecting eschatologist would dream of damning his fellows for his own unworth. It is not only unprofessional, but a violation of the principle of parsimony, since like as not, his fellows have already been damned. But if a rare exception is sometimes necessary, then any damning that a responsible eschatologist will do, will be based solely on the unworth of his fellows, not his own. As for his own unworth, it is of little moment here. It is best to treat it as a purely private matter so as not to awaken prurient interests in the reader.

Eschatologists exist only because they are needed. Most of them would rather be cab drivers, but they feel a responsibility. Cynics they are not.

Finally, and most serious of all, is the charge that eschatologists are aloof, transcendent, above it all, and disdain to participate in the ordinary life of mankind. What poppycock! Eschatologists are *engagé*. They are the only ones who take seriously what they see and smell around them. They never pretend to transcend it, any more than it is seemly for an inhabitant of Los Angeles to pretend to see through the smog. Moreover, they think affectations to transcendence have had more than a little to do with causing the present higher blindness. They believe that people should take to heart the fate of the philosopher Heidegger, who might have been a great eschatologist save for a tragic propensity to dabble in transcendence. In 1930 he wrote with eschatological insight that evokes envy even today:

> The spiritual decline of the earth is so far advanced
> that the nations are in danger of losing the last bit of
> spiritual energy that makes it possible to see the decline
> and to appraise it as such.[9]

And then, as if he had single-handedly to ensure the transcendent truth of his own statement—something an experienced eschatologist would never do—Heidegger applauded Adolf Hitler four years later. Some years after that, still seeking transcendence, he retired to a mountaintop in the Black Forest. After spending a few years in the forest, he came out and said:

> The essence of Enframing is that setting-upon
> gathered in itself which entraps the truth of its own

[9]Martin Heidegger, *Introduction to Metaphysics*, trans. Ralph Manheim (New Haven: Yale University Press, 1959), p. 38.

coming to presence with oblivion.[10]

Eschatologists may be quacks. But they are neither cynics, nor romantics, nor do they claim transcendence. They do claim to know one, thing, however. And what they know is this. A desert is not a Holiday Inn, and the survivors of the higher learning are not tourists passing through on their way to Vegas, no matter what mirages may parade before their feverish minds. The survivor-eschatologist knows these mirages well. He has, at one time or another, chased them all.

But, it is fitting to ask, how then does the survivor survive, and for what?

It has been truly said that truth spread by propaganda is a lie. By the same token hope spread by publication may be despair. Nevertheless the reader is entitled to an answer. And perhaps this much may be encouragingly said. An eschatologist knows that a desert may have its own peculiar charms for the one who comes to terms with it. Certainly, the sparse life that appears there is somehow more alive than life around the swimming pool at the Holiday Inn. The survivor also knows, as he wanders through the trackless waste, that there are occasional patches of shade and sources of water, though he cannot predict when and where he may stumble across them, let alone direct a tourist from Wisconsin to them.

The best thing of all, of course, is when two survivors who know they are survivors chance upon the same shady place at the same time. Then they may talk and laugh and enjoy each other's silence betweentimes. And they will share their meager provisions in the gathering twilight. That is all there is. At least it is all that may be safely said. But it is enough.

Anyone who cares to pursue the subject further will find it listed in the catalogue under "Eschatology Department." Most students are well advised to begin with the following course:

Eschatology 11

An Introduction to Desert Survival
A Non-credit course for the general student.

A study of the flora and fauna of the North American Edenic desert. Topics to be considered include: mi-

---

[10]Martin Heidegger, "The Turning" in *The Question Concerning Technology and Other Essays*, trans. William Lovitt (New York: Harper & Row, 1977), p. 36.

rages and what to do about them, snakebite and how to live with it, and communicating with tourists. Special emphasis will be placed on problem-solving and the afterlife. Survivors will learn how to recognize each other.

The Arts That Liberate: Labeling the Black Box

Adrienne Bond

There is an old story that is often used in discussions of what we refer to as a liberal arts education. An old farmer who was sending his son to college at great personal sacrifice was asked, "Why send the boy off to get an expensive education if he's coming back to the farm?" The old man replied, "I want him to have Homer to think about while he's plowing."

If we substitute Virgil or Shakespeare or Milton for Homer, the story's meaning changes very little, which makes us suspect that the liberal arts education is not a matter of specific content. Indeed, a committee planning a liberal arts core curriculum might allow a student to select from one of these writers, choose between art and music, and complete a sequence of courses in his choice of sciences. A student who masters French is as well regarded as one who masters German or, for that matter, Latin or Greek.

If a liberal arts curriculum does not consist of specific content or information, if two students can receive equally good educations without taking one course in common, then the first step in understanding its value may call for a black box. Gregory Bateson explains this concept as follows:

> A "black box" is a conventional agreement between scientists to stop trying to explain things at a certain point . . . a temporary agreement. . . . It's a word that comes from the engineers. When they draw a diagram of a complicated machine, they use a sort of shorthand. Instead of drawing all the details, they put a box to stand for a whole bunch of parts and label the box with what that bunch of parts is supposed to *do*.[1]

The purpose of this paper, then, is to try to *label the box*, to determine what the liberal arts education is trying to *do* that makes it more important and at the same time more difficult to provide each year.

There is a very old story in Genesis which explains the variety of languages in the world as a consequence of the building of a great city and a tower intended to reach up to heaven.

> And the Lord said, Behold, the people is one, and they have all one language . . . and now nothing will be restrained from them which they have imagined to do. Go to, let us go down and there confound their languages that they might not understand one another's speech. So the Lord scattered them abroad from thence upon the face of all the earth, and they left off to build the city (Gen. 11:6-8).

Today the development of a nomadic tribe into a race of city builders and their subsequent decline and dispersal might be explained as follows:

> Technological changes lead to "the loss of the eternal verities and the fixed order, the weakening of traditions and institutions, the shifting values, the altered patterns of relationships,"[2] and these changes occasion substantial changes in language.

---

[1] Gregory Bateson, *Steps to an Ecology of Mind* (New York: Ballantine, 1972), pp. 39-40.

[2] Allen Wheelis, *The Quest for Identity* (New York: Norton, 1958), p. 83.

The second version quoted above is certainly not a "translation" of the first. It is more like a parallel answer to the same question. The differences in the answers exist because over the years the process described above has occurred in our own culture; and as a consequence we tend to use expository form and an objective vocabulary now rather than telling a story, not because we prefer to or choose to but because it's what we can do. Walter Benjamin uses another story from the Old Testament to illustrate this change. He differentiates between "Paradisic" language which is a language of perfect and immediate knowledge and "fallen" language which is endlessly differentiated, the "abyss of prattle."[3]

A language is an expression of a common view of reality and its vocabulary refers back to that view. The same pressures which change the way a group sees the world, cause the language to change gradually to fill new needs. New "languages" grow within the old one, like a set of nested boxes; and in our rapidly changing, literate society a number of these "nested languages" now coexist. These are not foreign languages—they are all English—but, because of their diversity, many a frustrated committee has "left off to build the city."

In order to see how a liberal arts education helps us alleviate this situation we will look rather briefly at what some of these "languages" are and how they affect the individual and the accumulated recorded cultural material of our society.

If we stick to our metaphor of English as a set of "nested languages," the oldest and richest is (and this is true in every culture) a traditional vocabulary reflecting a mythical metaphysics. Anthropologists tell us that social behavior preceded both language and self-consciousness as we know it. This stage is what Grimm calls a *mythopoeic* age, wherein the basic behavior patterns of the group were acted out; primitive man lived his *mythos*. As language developed, this *mythos* was articulated and became a story with endless variations and episodes. This was the culture's way of explaining itself to itself and remembering what it was. We can see this process more clearly by looking at a specific tribal culture.

Our medium of communication, English, was originally an unwritten language called Anglo-Saxon. The Anglo-Saxon people possessed

---

[3]Walter Benjamin, *Reflections* (New York: Harcourt, Brace, Jovanovich, 1978), p. 328.

an extensive body of oral literature with many conventions or poetic "habits." For example, in their poetry the important words in each line began with the same letter. There were also groups of words called "kennings" to refer poetically to such things as the ocean (whale-road) or treasure (twisted gold). Conventions such as possession of magic swords, conferring of gold bracelets, and referrals to wolves and crows on the battlefield were traditional poetic devices which appeared in story after story. Each tribe had a poet called a *scop* (pronounced *schope*) who learned and recited the literature of his people.

One of the main duties of the *scop* or "Shaper" was to take each important new event and, by using the poetic devices mentioned above, modify the event so as to fit it into the tribal myth. As the song took shape the characters in the event/story became more vivid and larger than life, and their behavior was absorbed into an archetypal pattern. Ritually an important event was not completed—be it a military victory, a hunting accident, or a power struggle—until it had been incorporated into the tribe's body of legend.

Because of this steady subsumption of reality into myth, the image that a people had of itself changed very, very slowly. Time was viewed as cyclical with changes in details but reassuring repetition of basic roles, behavior, and events.

A metaphysics (religion, ideology, worldview) explains the nature of the world for us, places us in it and, in doing so, makes certain demands upon us. It does this through language. The medieval universe was earth-centered, with death and decay at the center. The material earth was surrounded by the spiritual sky, and time involved change on earth but was eternal in the heavens encircling it. Man, the link between the two realms, had both a spiritual nature which yearned toward the eternal and a material nature which weighed him down. In that world of hierarchies and dualities the dominant mode was narrative, and each person was a central character in "the story of man and the world according to the divine plan of salvation."[4] This transcendent story of spirit versus flesh, of good versus evil, acted itself out in literature through fixed types; as late as the early nineteenth century even "history could still be regarded as the Transcendent Idea realizing itself in the actual."[5]

---

[4] Carl L. Becker, *The Heavenly City of the Eighteenth Century Philosophers* (New Haven: Yale University Press, 1932), p. 17.

[5] Ibid., p. 18.

The impact of this notion of time and space on all of life is articulated in Brecht's *Galileo* by the little monk, who has looked through Galileo's telescope but has decided to repress what he has seen because of his parents' painfully impoverished lives.

They have been told that God relies upon them and that the pageant of the world has been written around them that they may be tested in the important or unimportant parts handed out to them. How could they take it, were I to tell them that they are on a lump of stone ceaselessly spinning in empty space, circling around a second-rate star?[6]

Man knew who he was and what was expected of him and had the entire universe focused on him as he went through each day's activities.

This mythic view of reality was expressed in a rich vocabulary in words heavy with meaning. A *creature* with a *purpose* has dimensions that an *organism* with a *function* does not. *Sublunary* has overtones that *terrestrial* lacks, and *redemption* makes *adjustment* seem pretty trivial. John Milton, the last Englishman to write an epic, was able to do so because he was able to work within this system. His use of time and space ignores the Copernican solar system (of which he was quite aware). *Paradise Lost* may be seen as a monument to a way of seeing what was thereafter inaccessible to serious writers; because of the change in our views of reality and a corresponding change in vocabulary the poem is now inaccessible to modern readers without an extensive system of footnotes. Aldous Huxley, in *The Doors of Perception*, quotes Walter Benjamin to point out that "the art of storytelling is reaching its end because the epic side of truth, wisdom, is dying out." The displacement of storytelling is "only a concomitant symptom of the secular productive forces of history, a concomitant that has quite gradually removed narrative from the realm of living speech."[7]

The change from a feudal system to a market system, from a mythic to a scientific world view, created a need for a comparatively objective vocabulary to express ideas for which the heavily freighted

---

6Bertolt Brecht, *Galileo* (New York: Grove Press, 1966), p. 83.

7Aldous Huxley, *The Doors of Perception* (New York: Harper & Row, 1963), p. 31.

traditional language was inappropriate. A culture of instrumentality requires an instrumental language and one slowly formed in response to the actual instances in which it was needed. This did not happen without resistance; whoever controls the language can limit what can be said. A dramatization of this conflict can be seen in Brecht's *Galileo*, in a scene where Galileo is trying to show the moons of Jupiter to a group of people who do not wish to encourage him.

> Voice of Philosopher: Quaedam miracula universi. Orbes mystice canorae, arcus crystallini, circulatio corporum coelestium. Cyclorum epicyclorumque intoxicatio, integritas tabulae chordarum et architectura elata globorum coelestium.
>
> Galileo: Shall we speak in everyday language? My colleague, Mr. Federzoni, does not understand Latin.
>
> Philosopher: Is it necessary that he should?

After some protest, the philosopher begins again in "everyday language":

> Philosopher: I was about to recall to Mr. Galileo some of the wonders of the universe as they are set down for us in the Divine Classics. Remind him of the "mystically musical spheres, the crystal arches, the circulation of the heavenly bodies—the intoxication of the cycles and epicycles, the integrity of the tables of chords, and the enraptured architecture of the celestial globes."
>
> Elderly lady: What diction!
>
> Philosopher: May I pose the question: Why should we go out of our way to look for things that can only strike a discord in the ineffable harmony?[8]

Obviously this is not a language which will admit any profitable discussion of Galileo's discoveries, and he leaves unsuccessful. The established thought of his day could "dismiss the recalcitrant fact in favor of the great idea." Now of course the balance is in the other direction, as Carl Becker says:

> The fact is that we have no first premise. Since Whirl is king, we must start with the whirl, the mess of things as presented in experience. We start with the irreducible brute fact, and

---

[8]Brecht, *Galileo*, p. 66.

we must take it as we find it, since it is no longer permitted to
coax or cajole it, hoping to fit it into some or other category
of thought on the assumption that the pattern of the world is
a logical one. Accepting the fact as given, we observe it,
experiment with it, verify it, classify it, measure it if possible,
and reason about it as little as may be.

Since our supreme object is to measure and master the
world, we can make relatively little use of theology, philosophy and deductive logic—the three stately entrance ways to
knowledge erected in the Middle Ages. In the course of eight
centuries these disciplines have fallen from their high estate,
and in their place we have enthroned history, science and the
technique of observation and measurement.[9]

In the last century the traditional metaphysics continued to be
dislodged in a fragmentary fashion by a variety of deterministic theories. The ideas of Marx and Darwin seemed to provide a sort of
metaphysics and to place man in a new relationship with nature, but
the quality of the social and political behavior that grew out of this
metaphysics left something to be desired. As these ideas changed from
the content of nineteenth century thought to the basic assumptions of
modern thought, their special vocabularies became firmly fixed in the
language.

Having inherited the tongues of men and of angels, the present
generation would seem to be the most articulate of people. Why then
do we find ourselves, more and more, using such impoverished terms
as *adjustment, guilt-trip, role-model, life-style, acting out, sexually
active, conflict,* or *meaningful relationship?* Alasdair MacIntyre has
this to say:

It is the vocabulary of Jules Feiffer's characters. It is also the
vocabulary of Feiffer's readers: the vocabulary of a segment
of urban, middle-class intelligentsia whose cultural situation
deprived them of large-scale theory at the same time as it
made large-scale theory an intense necessity for them. The
skepticism of an earlier generation had deprived them of
religion. The history of their own time deprived them of
Marxism and in so doing of their hold upon the public world

---

[9]Becker, *The Heavenly City*, pp. 16-17.

of political ends. The intellectual may be socially valued for his functional utility; but otherwise, his arena is increasingly that of private life. He needs to make his own experience intelligible: an image of the public world as a mere projection upon a larger screen of the private rages and longings, hopes and fears which circumscribe him. The intolerable character of his condemnation to private life is relieved by an overpersonalization of that life. The ideology of personal relationships invokes a public sanction in the closed system of psychoanalytic theory. And a whole vocabulary of personal relationships enables psychoanalysis to appear, not as one more questionable theory, but as the unquestionable framework which gives life meaning.[10]

He goes on to charge that there is "no discipline to compare with psychoanalysis for the way in which the very use of the vocabulary commits the novice—quite unconsciously—to acceptance of a complex theoretical framework."[11] As we found Galileo and his mechanic unable to communicate a scientific fact in mythical language, we now find people unable to express notions of good and evil because of the nature of the words they use.

Several years ago a freshman English class at Mercer was reading a short story, "A Good Man is Hard to Find," by Flannery O'Connor, in which an escaped convict kills a family of tourists whose car has broken down on a country road. A student struggled with the apparent lack of motivation for this act and finally said, "It doesn't really look like the man is mentally ill, so I guess he has to be a victim of society." The author had taken great pains to make it clear that the "Misfit" *knew* that the killing was evil and *chose* to do it. The student had no language for dealing with the situation from this perspective. As MacIntyre puts it, "in our ordinary secular vocabulary we have no language to express common needs, hopes, and fears that go beyond the immediacies of technique and social structure."[12]

O'Connor herself was aware of the problem she faced communi-

---

[10]Alasdair MacIntyre, *Against the Self-Images of the Age* (Notre Dame: University of Notre Dame Press, 1971), p. 35.

[11]Ibid., p. 29.

[12]Ibid., p. 23.

cating with a public whose basic metaphysics was different from hers. In "The Fiction Writer and His Country" she says:

> The novelist with Christian concerns will find in modern life distortions which are repugnant to him, and his problem will be to make these appear as distortions to an audience which is used to seeing them as natural; and he may well be forced to take ever more violent means to get his vision across to this hostile audience.[13]

Bridging this gap involves the author's walking a thin line between speaking in the tongues of angels and losing his audience, or speaking in the tongues of men and losing his message. Alasdair MacIntyre discusses the problem as follows:

> The theologians begin from orthodoxy, but the orthodoxy which has learned from Kierkegaard and Barth becomes too easily a closed circle, in which believer speaks only to believer, in which all human content is concealed. Turning aside from this arid in-group theology, the most perceptive theologians wish to translate what they have to say to an atheistic world. But they are doomed to one of two failures. Either they suceed in their translation: in which case what they find themselves saying has been transformed into the atheism of their hearers. Or they fail in their translation: in which case no one hears what they have to say but themselves.[14]

Flannery O'Connor continues her explanation of the use of the grotesque in her stories:

> When you can assume that your audience holds the same beliefs you do, you can relax a little and use more normal means of talking to it; when you have to assume that it does not, then you have to make your vision apparent by shock— to the hard of hearing you shout, and for the almost-blind you draw large and startling figures.[15]

---

[13]Flannery O'Connor, "The Fiction Writer and His Country," *Mystery and Manners* (New York: Farrar, Straus & Giroux, 1969), pp. 33-34.

[14]MacIntyre, *Against the Self-Images*, pp. 19-20.

[15]O'Connor, "The Fiction Writer," p. 34.

The failure of the movie, *Wise Blood*, to communicate to any except the initiates into O'Connor's work, shows that a modern audience may merely assume that the shock *is* the message. Robert Bolt discusses the limits of this approach in theater:

> Each time it is done it is a little less unexpected, so that a bigger and bigger dosage will be needed to produce the same effect. If it were continued indefinitely it would finally not be unexpected at all. The theatrical convention would then have been entirely dissipated and we should have in the theatre a situation with one person, who used to be an actor, desperately trying to engage the attention—by rude gestures, loud noises, indecent exposure, fireworks, anything— of other persons, who used to be the audience. As this point was approached some very lively evenings might be expected, but the depth and subtlety of the notions which can be communicated by such methods may be doubted.[16]

We have looked at the difficulty of the author in being understood by an audience whose language and metaphysics are different. The *scop* we looked at earlier in this essay had no such problem. There was one reality and he maintained it, but this is not possible today. Similarly the stress on the reader or observer whose language is inadequate or whose reality is shaky is considerable. In *Slaughterhouse-Five*, Kurt Vonnegut offers us a character who is presented with a variety of simultaneous verbal realities which are seemingly unconnected:

> While on maneuvers in South Carolina, Billy played hymns we knew from childhood, played them on a little black organ which . . . had thirty-nine keys and two stops— *vox humana* and *vox celeste*. . . .
>
> One time on maneuvers Billy was playing "A Mighty Fortress is Our God," with music by Johann Sebastian Bach and words by Martin Luther. It was Saturday morning. Billy and his chaplain had gathered a congregation of about fifty soldiers on a Carolina hillside. An umpire appeared. . . .
>
> The umpire had comical news. The congregation had been theoretically spotted from the air by a theoretical enemy. They were all theoretically dead, now. . . .

---

[16]Robert Bolt, *A Man For All Seasons* (New York: Vintage Press, 1966), p. xvi.

Toward the end of maneuvers, Billy was given emergency furlough home because his father . . . was shot dead by a friend while they were out hunting deer.[17] Billy is then sent to the front where he is befriended by Roland Weary, a young soldier who tries to be an epic hero in a modern war and dies from an infected blister. Billy, an inarticulate young man for whom both *vox humana* and *vox celeste* are incomprehensible, responds to the confusion by retreating into a fantasy world. Billy Pilgrim's dilemma is the dilemma of modern man. Wallace Stevens in "The Noble Rider and the Sound of Words" says:

All the great things have been denied and we live in an intricacy of new and local mythologies, political, economic, poetic, which are asserted with an ever-enlarging incoherence.[18]

In an age when many people find it increasingly difficult to articulate an essential order and use it to shape the events of their lives, the task of the writer is more difficult and more important than ever. Flannery O'Connor says "We live now in an age which doubts both fact and value, which is swept this way and that by momentary convictions. Instead of reflecting a balance from the world around him, the novelist now has to achieve one from a felt balance inside himself."[19] This balance for O'Connor comes from her religious convictions and she creates her stories by forcing the events of a secular society into the traditional structure of good versus evil. The distortions that this creates make clear the grotesque nature of much of modern life.

Kurt Vonnegut, on the other hand, presents life as a mixture of conflicting disfunctional myths which confuse and torment modern man, who would like to be good but never quite knows what is going on. Vonnegut, who was educated to be a chemist, cannot accept the apparent lack of moral order in the world; he is immensely popular among young people because he articulates for them their outrage at what they perceive as meaninglessness in modern society. Both of these authors are attempting to deal with spiritual matters in a secular

[17]Kurt Vonnegut, *Slaughterhouse-Five* (New York: Delta, 1969), pp. 26-27.

[18]Wallace Stevens, "The Noble Rider and the Sound of Words," in *Modern Poetics*, ed. James Scully (New York: McGraw-Hill, 1965), p. 134.

[19]O'Connor, "The Fiction Writer," p. 49.

language. Their popularity testifies to the public's need for such attempts to be made.

Matthew Arnold predicted that the role of poetry in the twentieth century would be to replace religion. This challenge was picked up by Wallace Stevens who maintained that the poet has to try to do this, but that he has also to realize that he cannot. Whereas a mythical world view includes a Golden Age in the past or outside of time, and a utopian vision of progressive man includes a Golden Age in the future, the modern poet can produce at best a few transitory golden moments. He is, in Stevens' words, "A metaphysician in the dark, twanging / An instrument, twanging a wiry string that gives / Sounds passing through sudden rightnesses. . . ."[20] An examination of a short poem by Stevens will demonstrate one of these "rightnesses."

Anecdote of the Jar

I placed a jar in Tennessee
And round it was, upon a hill.
It made the slovenly wilderness
Surround that hill.

The wilderness rose up to it,
And sprawled around, no longer wild.
The jar was round upon the ground
And tall and of a port in air.

It took dominion everywhere.
The jar was grey and bare
It did not give of bird or bush,
Like nothing else in Tennessee.[21]

In the first stanza of this poem the human mind creates order through a work of art, the jar; it creates a "port" at which all may enter into its organization. Similarly, Richard Palmer expands on Heidegger's description of a Greek temple as an "open space in being":

To put the matter in Heidegger's ontological terms, it is so with every great work of art: it creates, through its form, a

---

[20] *The Collected Poems of Wallace Stevens* (New York: Alfred A. Knopf, 1954); used by permission of the publisher.

[21] Ibid., p. 249.

world in which being comes to stand. Being is encountered in understanding not as a discrete entity but as a part of a unity, in relation to the horizon of understanding or what may be called "world."[22]

In the second stanza as the organization extends itself and imposes its circularity, it causes the wilderness to "surround" it, "sprawl around" until it takes "dominion everywhere." But even as this happens the light goes out of the poem in the remaining three lines. The jar is "grey and bare" and dead; unlike the world it seemed momentarily to make orderly it has no "bird or bush," no color, no light. The "sudden rightness" is gone even before the poem ends.

Gregory Bateson tells us that it is essential to "have a conceptual system which will force us to see the 'message' (e.g., the art object) as *both* itself internally patterned and itself a part of a larger patterned universe.[23] He doesn't tell us how to maintain this beyond the aesthetic moment. The modern poet has lost his battle against chaos; things fall apart. The contemporary poet records his perception of this defeat, and the critics work on the methodology of the failure of order.

John Gardner begins his book, *On Moral Fiction*, with a story from Norse mythology which goes something like this: In the olden days Odin used to stride around Middle Earth fighting back the enemies of order. At one point it seemed that chaos was closing in, and Odin went to the king of the Trolls for advice. The king said, "I'll tell you the secret of victory but you'll have to give me your left eye."

"These are desperate times," said Odin, and he plucked out his eye and handed it over. "Now what's the secret of keeping chaos from overwhelming us?" he said.

"Watch with both eyes," said the troll.[24]

In one sense or another all times are desperate times, and like Odin, we are always in danger of seeing less than we need to see. We have let the trolls get control of one eye—the one which mediates *information*, and we have forgotten how to use the other—the one which mediates *experience*. A liberal arts education will certainly not exempt us from

---

[22]Richard E. Palmer, *Hermeneutics* (Evanston: Northwestern University Press, 1969), p. 239.

[23]Bateson, *Steps to an Ecology of Mind*, p. 132.

[24]John Gardner, *On Moral Fiction* (New York: Basic Books, 1977).

the battle against chaos, but ideally it should give us the ability to see what is going on a little more clearly.

First, let us consider information since this is an age of the language of facts. Information is always already mediated when we receive it. Almost invariably information is conveyed in language, which is our principal mediating device. Information is mediated before the gathering process when someone decides what information is needed. Information is mediated by the *way* it is gathered, the methodology; it is mediated by the way it is interpreted. The decision to release parts of the information or even to release the existence of the information is mediation. If it is to be broadcast, word choice and tone of voice mediate it. These are the *facts* of our world. Consider, for example, the difficulties of making a responsible personal decision on our role in El Salvador. Or what soap to buy. Or whom to vote for. Or how to invest our savings. The trolls have our eye and we have to ask them what is out there, even in a society where the press is free. Chaos closes in.

What does a liberal arts education do to help us recover our ability to perceive, to make sense? To begin with we can learn how information is gathered, processed, and communicated by studying the sciences and social sciences. We can become more sensitive to the words with which information is expressed. When a new secretary of state makes a policy statement on human rights, "There will be no de-emphasis but a change in priority," we can see past the vigor and self-confidence and know that he is talking nonsense, that he knows he is talking nonsense, and that he assumes that we will not know the difference. These are important things for us to know.

One of the important aspects of the language of facts is the way language has to be stripped down in order to handle information at all efficiently. Words must become value-free, culture-free, and free of assumptions and connotations, or they will clog the machinery. This leaves the affective domain free to riot through the language unhampered by the weight of specificity. A pizza chain has as its motto "We give you more of the things you love." This motto was brought to my attention by two liberal arts students at Mercer. I like to think that their education made them aware of the manipulative nature of this vacuous statement.

If information is mediated for us by others through language, a liberal arts education should help liberate us from manipulation by improving our own ability to understand and use language. Richard Palmer says:

> Language is not man's means of putting wordless thoughts and wordless experience into a form to which he has assigned a meaning; thinking, understanding, and experience are all completely linguistic, for it is through language that one has the world of understanding in and through which objects take their place in his experience.[25]

Trivial language condemns us to trivial thoughts.

Another motto which may be heard on television says: "This is who we are and what we do." This is an especially catchy motto because it brings us to the other area of understanding: the ability to order and communicate our own experience. Traditionally our experience has been mediated through heuristic metaphors (who we are) and by myths or stories (what we do). The trolls have not preempted this way of seeing; no one has. It is practically defunct. One of the ways in which chaos or lack of order threatens modern man most directly is through his inability to interpret or understand his own experience. That understanding is no longer informed by shared myths and metaphors.

One of my favorite mementos is a letter I got from one of my children who was away at camp. It read "Dear Mom, They won't let us go for free swim until we write home. Love, Ernie." A child's experience at play is so directly perceived, so immediate, that we do not expect an articulate account. More and more, however, we encounter adults who, at the end of a vacation, can only tell you what their gas mileage was; or who, when asked what they do, tell us where they do it. "I work at Sears" or "I'm with C & S." The old discrete models for being—scholar, lady, storyteller, gentleman, wise man, faithful retainer, prophet, or hero—are only dimly remembered. And the images that are offered now are too transitory to model a life around: how dated are G. I. Joe, hippie, organization man, peace marcher; how soon will "good old boy" or "preppie" be last year's throwaway metaphors?

The myths or stories which give meaning to the individual life in time—the young man who seeks his fortune, the poor girl whose virtue wins her a marriage to the king's son, or the clever pig who outwits the

---

[25] Palmer, *Hermeneutics*, p. 230.

wolf, for example—are still around as artifacts but no longer serve even as literary models. The rites of passage, the quests, the visits to the underworld, are lost to us. Freshmen in college now rarely know Bible stories or Greek myths, and know only the fairy tales and children's stories which have been made into television cartoons. They know no nursery rhymes at all. How can we as a learning community help them mediate their experience?

The liberal arts education can, by teaching the literature of the Greeks, of the Elizabethans, of Conrad or Faulkner, show the student the possibility of significance of human behavior-in-time, of the actual occurrence of what Faulkner called the "old universal truths of the human heart . . . love, honor, pride, pity, compassion and sacrifice." A student once told me she had never been able to make any sense out of the Patty Hearst case until she read *Sanctuary*. Experience, to be comprehensible, must be mediated by the individual; consequently a liberal arts education should offer a repertoire of models for understanding experience in valid and meaningful ways. The quality of our experience is dependent on the quality of ideas and images we have learned: people who know *Romeo and Juliet* perceive "love" differently from people who watch *Love Boat*.

One of the ways we learn is by finding a teacher. Early in life we learn by watching behavior and modeling ourselves accordingly. Later we learn through language, and eventually we can learn ideas and methods through a teacher without getting to know the teacher at all. There is a sort of bonding phenomenon that happens occasionally where the two are combined and students imitate not only the ideas but even the dress and mannerisms of their mentors. One of the things one hopes a good education will do is to help the student find such teachers and then learn to distinguish between compelling ideas and a compelling personality, between the metaphor and the man: whether a strong person offers a puny idea or an inadequate person has valuable insights, either a good example or a good insight is too rare to reject.

Occasionally a book goes round the campus here that excites general interest, because an author has brought some area of human life or thought into the light and out of disarray in some useful way. Expecting him to be an apotheosis, an embodiment of his clear idea, we will invite the author to campus. We usually are disappointed. When a man has gone to the edge of the world and spread out his mind like a great net to catch some elusive idea, often what we see is what is left of him after he has done that. When Faulkner was invited to Stockholm to accept the Nobel Prize he wanted to stay at home. He said that the prize was for his work, and that what was left of *him* after 30 years' effort "wasn't worth dragging over there." Often we are so disappointed at the discrepancy between the offering and the offerer that we come close to being rude. Education helps us overcome this. Few of us can live up to our best visions, and the reason we try to realize them in language is because we know that we ourselves will change, will forget.

Education also helps students build defenses against the person who, through force of personality, would seek to invalidate another's way of mediating experience by shifting the modality, significance, content, or vocabulary in which it is expressed. Man needs a variety of approaches to truth because truth can only be *approached*, not ascertained. A liberal arts education should provide a variety of approaches.

There are several new books out now extolling the "interpretive community." Here again the quality of the community experience is dependent upon the quality of the ideas, concepts, metaphors, or myths that underlie it. An interpretive community built on a narrow view of man can produce impoverished ideas and oppressive interaction, and can limit the growth of individual members. The humanities can furnish a broad and generous and liberating base especially when the emphasis is on content rather than methodology because it provides a narrative structure for experience rather than reducing it to some mechanical model.

The interpretive community is built around a shared way of mediation. Dietrich Bonhoeffer discusses the difference between a community based on the authority of a system of belief and one based on human personality.

> Within the spiritual community there is never, nor in any way any "immediate" relationship of one to another, whereas human community expresses a profound, elemental, human desire for community, for immediate contact with other souls, . . . whether this occur in the union of love or what is after all the same thing, in the forcing of another person into one's sphere of power and influence. Here is where the humanly strong person is in his element, securing for himself the admiration, the love, or the fear of the weak. Here human ties, suggestions, and bonds are everything, and in the immediate community of souls we have reflected

144 / *Perspectives on Liberal Education*

the distorted image of everything that is originally and solely peculiar to community mediated through Christ.[26]

Ideally one would like to think of the university as a whole as an "interpretive community" sharing some basic views of man and reality and a common vocabulary for communicating these. This is, however, by no means the case. It would be accurate, I think, to describe the liberal arts college as a number of overlapping interpretive communities which alternatively attract and repel one another and occasionally merge.

The liberal arts curriculum provides for today's students to participate in a variety of learning groups, and to learn a variety of vocabularies. The apprehension of the physical world involves sophisticated ways of weighing, measuring, counting, analyzing, testing, and categorizing data. The student who does not wish to master these skills is acquainted at least with the methods of science and social science and can appreciate their strengths and limitations when he is presented with mediated information.

Through the humanities the liberal arts student is acquainted with the myths and metaphors which earlier cultures have used to inform experience. Many, perhaps most, of these are no longer of use to us today because of our present perception of reality and self. The great ideas can no longer eclipse the recalcitrant facts. It is vitally important, however, that we be aware that such things existed once and could exist again, and that if we cannot use the models of the past directly, we can use them as models for models.

The liberal arts student, then, works in both informational and experiential modes; ideally he achieves some synthesis by analogy, by subordination or by some dynamic tension between the private reality of perception and that vast world of past and future, of values and ideas, the community reality of language. The battle against chaos goes on and on; if we "watch with both eyes" we may, at least, have a degree of depth to our vision.

Freud said that to be healthy a person must be able to work and love. A healthy liberal arts college provides opportunities and models for work and love. To create or discover order is honorable work. To use common words to give away our creations and discoveries, rather

---

[26]Deitrich Bonhoeffer, *Life Together* (New York: Harper & Row, 1954), pp. 32-33.

than using arcane words to brand them as our own, is an expression of love. Both enlarge the interpretive community. Perhaps we can label our "black box" now, even if we're not sure how it works: *a device for enlarging the student's interpretive community through work and through love.*

"New Students" in Liberal Arts Colleges: Threat or Challenge?

Marjorie T. Davis and Charles C. Schroeder

Faculty nationwide agree that today's students are different. These students do not stage protests or bomb buildings; they dress neatly and seem more polite, more serious. Yet somehow the gap between students and faculty may be wider than it was in the sixties: Where are the ideals, the dreams? Where are the students eager to talk all night about moral or philosophic issues? Faculty are sometimes heard to complain, "All these students want is the diploma—they don't care about learning anything."

Some educational observers, like Patricia Cross, have suggested that these different college populations—these "New Students"—may present an unprecedented challenge to education as it is commonly perceived in small liberal arts colleges. The New Students are not well prepared to deal with liberal arts courses. They seem economically motivated, uncommitted to the inherent worth of liberal learning, and apathetic about contemporary issues. Some observers say that these New Students threaten the very existence of the liberal arts—that in their consumer-like search for higher salaries and secure careers, they encourage colleges to adopt the Madison Avenue sell where the slickest brochures, lowest demands, and best-trained admissions counselors have the greatest impact on institutional survival. Everyone realizes by now that the available supply of eighteen-year-olds is rapidly declining; that inflation eats away at institutional endowments and revenues; and that the focus on survival is rapidly replacing the interest in liberal education. But these things exist in some conceptual level removed from daily awareness. Students exist in the immediate reality. They sit in classrooms daily before faculty who look out at blank eyes, who fail to get a response to brilliant lectures or exciting concepts. Students are the one ingredient in the college setting that cannot be ignored or dismissed. No matter how good the liberal arts product, faculty can't sell it if students aren't buying.

Does this New Student constitute the greatest threat ever to the survival of small liberal arts colleges? Must faculty devise endless remedial programs, sacrifice standards, and abandon the traditional goals of liberal education just to survive?

We think not. We believe that liberal learning remains viable today, that it is perhaps even more necessary in the 1980s than it was in Cardinal Newman's day. The question, then, is how to promote the traditional values of the liberal arts to a non-traditional body of students. We do not need to design a model for mass education; rather, we need to redirect our focus to the individuals we are educating. If we can learn who our students are and how they see the world, then we can learn to translate our perceptions in ways that will succeed. We can, in short, turn the threat of New Students into a challenge.

Let us begin by taking a closer look at the New Students. Who are they? What things do they do well or poorly? What do they want and expect from college? Then let us take a look at liberal arts colleges as they are presently designed and staffed. What are faculty like? What things do they do well? What do they expect from the institution and from their students? Once we gain insight into some of the challenges, we will suggest some strategies for coping with these challenges and some forecasts about the long-range effects on educational institutions and society.

The Rising Number of New Students

College enrollments have more than doubled since 1960, largely as a result of an egalitarian movement to open the doors of higher education to the masses. Federal regulations have removed many traditional barriers to handicapped, economically disadvantaged, and minority students. Generous funding has been responsible for ever larger numbers of students entering college; financial aid has increased 6,000 percent in the last twenty-five years.[1] Because of increased access to post-secondary education, students now enter colleges often with very little understanding of what college is all about. They may be relatively uninformed and unmotivated. They come through the open doors, however, with very high expectations about what benefits they will derive from a college degree.

Although students have always valued the economic promises associated with a college degree, New Students enter higher education *primarily* to obtain a better job and higher socioeconomic status. These students expect their college experience to emphasize vocational training and develop practical skills directly applicable to the world of work. They often do not expect, or even want, the traditional academic experience.[2]

Not only do New Students expect vocational training, they also expect a significant amount of personal attention from faculty, administrators, and their peers. New Students expect colleges to provide a wide array of programs and services that will remove the obstacles to obtaining a degree; thus they expect, and often demand, more academic support services, financial aid, career counseling, and special programs.[3]

Although many educators might suppose that New Students are predominantly black, Cross indicates that the majority are Caucasian, first-generation college students. They often come from families where both parents work in blue collar jobs. Whereas most freshmen entering

---

[1]K. Patricia Cross, *Accent on Learning* (San Francisco: Jossey-Bass Inc., 1976), p. 8

[2]Ibid., p. 7.

[3]Adrienne Barna, James Haws, and L. Lee Knefelkamp, "The New Student: Challenge to Student Affairs," unpublished paper included in *Selected Papers on the Learning Process,* for Mercer University Conference, 1980, p. 7.

college in the late fifties or early sixties scored in the upper quartile, New Students score in the second and third quartiles on high school grades and college entrance examinations.[4]

New Students differ from traditional students not only in expectations and preparation for college, but also in academic values and learning styles. Since New Students see education as a means to a better life, they are not interested in learning for learning's sake. Their motivation for education is predominantly extrinsic. In her book *Accent on Learning,* Cross describes the typical learning styles of New Students. They often lack confidence in their intellectual abilities and feel particularly uncomfortable with abstract ideas. On the Omnibus Personality Inventory, they consistently score lower than traditional students on scales measuring theoretical orientation, analytical and critical thinking, and autonomy. These results suggest, says Cross, that New Students have difficulty with complex concepts and ambiguity, are less independent in thought and judgement, and are more dependent on the wishes and ideas of those in authority. Compared to their more traditional predecessors, they are more passive, have less tolerance for diversity, are more dependent on immediate gratification, and exhibit more difficulties with basic reading and writing skills. They prefer highly structured situations and like to have things explained rather than figuring them out by themselves.[5]

Although the relationship is highly speculative, we are struck by the similarities between the characteristics of New Students as described by Cross, and students entering Mercer University from 1978 to 1980. Entering Mercer students were asked to complete a questionnaire on which they rated the relative importance of ten statements describing the purpose of education. They consistently rated vocational training highest. "Developing your understanding of such subjects as philosophy, art, literature, and music" received the lowest rating among the ten items. The second highest rating was given to the item "Developing your ability to get along with different kinds of people." They were also asked to rate the items of highest concern to them. Over ninety percent indicated that they were greatly concerned about surviving the academic challenge, deciding on a major or career, and developing the

---

[4]Cross, *Accent on Learning,* p. 6.

[5]Ibid., pp. 123-25.

ability to make friends. Also striking is the fact that ninety-one percent of these entering freshmen expected "help and support" from the faculty.[6]

When the same institutional research instrument was administered at the end of the freshman year to a stratified random sample of the freshman class, the results were quite similar. After a year in the liberal arts college, students persisted in rating vocational training highest and humanities lowest in importance—in fact, the numbers changed only one percentage point. Although the strength of their major concerns showed some decline, students continued to express concern for academic survival, career choices, and making friends. The only significant differences between the scores on entrance and the scores after one year were related to the faculty; students perceived significantly less support, encouragement, and involvement with faculty than they had originally expected.[7] Obviously, Mercer students sound much like New Students when they respond to questions about the purposes and concerns for their college education.

Data obtained from two other instruments supply further support for the comparison between Mercer students and Cross's New Students. The Myers-Briggs Type Indicator, a widely used instrument based on Jungian typology, was administered routinely to entering freshmen from 1978 through 1980; a total of 1,078 students took the instrument. The results indicate that approximately sixty percent of them prefer what the MBTI calls the *sensing* mode of perceiving, compared to forty percent who prefer the *intuitive* mode.[8] The learning styles of those who prefer sensing are characterized by a preference for direct, concrete experiences, moderate to high degrees of structure, linear learning, and often a need to know why before doing something. In general, sensing types prefer the concrete, the practical, and the immediate. They focus their perceptions primarily on the physical world. Contrast these learning styles to those of the intuitives. They are

[6]Charles C. Schroeder and David H. Kalsbeek, "Student Perceptions of the Purpose of College Education," Vol. 1, no. 1 from the Center for Research and Evaluation on Student Life (Mercer University: December, 1980), pp. 1-11.

[7]Ibid.

[8]Charles C. Schroeder, unpublished research, Mercer University. For complete information on the MBTI, see Myers, I. B., *Myers-Briggs Type Indicator: Manual* (Princeton NJ: Educational Testing Service, 1962).

generally global learners who prefer to focus their perceptions on imaginative possibilities rather than on concrete realities. Intuitives love the world of concepts, ideas, and abstractions. They prefer open-ended instruction to highly structured instruction, and they usually demonstrate a high degree of autonomy in their learning.[9]

A second instrument, the Omnibus Personality Inventory, was given to approximately 200 freshmen in the fall of 1980. Scores on this instrument used to assess student attitudes, values, and interests were compared to type preferences. It is interesting to note that students who prefer sensing scored lower than intuitives on scales measuring theoretical orientation and autonomy, but higher than intuitives on practical orientation.[10] Data from both the Myers-Briggs Type Indicator and the Omnibus Personality Inventory thus suggest further similarities between Mercer students (who are similar in most respects to students at other small, liberal arts colleges) and those Cross identifies as New Students.

We can't help but wonder whether there is a strong link between students described as sensors and the New Students. Is it not possible that a student's preferred mode of learning heavily influences performance on any academic measures, but especially on standardized tests? A review of thirty years of research on the Myers-Briggs suggests some theoretical relationships. In research conducted by Educational Testing Service in the early 1960s, for example, the mean SAT verbal ability score was forty-seven points higher for intuitives than for sensors.[11] Although it might be easy to assume that these differences indicate different intelligence levels, the evidence does not support this

---

[9]Gordon Lawrence, *People Types and Tiger Stripes: A Practical Guide to Learning Styles* (Gainesville, FL: Center for the Applications of Psychological Type, Inc., 1979), p. 6.

[10]Schroeder and Kalsbeek, unpublished research, Mercer University. For complete information on the OPI, see Paul Heist and George Yonge, *Omnibus Personality Inventory: Manual* (New York: The Psychological Corporation, 1968).

[11]J. Ross, "Progress Report on the College Student Characteristics Study" (Research Memorandum 61-11) *E T S Developments* (June 1961): 51. A more recent study of Mercer University freshmen (1980-1981) not only confirms this data, but also suggests significant differences on the quantitative scores as well as on the verbal. In the Mercer comparison, IN's scored sixty-eight points higher on the verbal portion than did ES's, and sixty-five points higher on the quantitative portion. (Schroeder and Kalsbeek, unpublished research, Mercer University.)

hypothesis. In general, sensing students tend to do just as well as intuitive students on aptitude tests that are not timed. Sensing students take longer to read questions, often going over them several times, whereas intuitives tend to respond immediately.[12] The difference in scores would seem to be related to the way they take tests, not to intelligence.

Educators might be led to question why so many of these sensors are entering college. The reason is fairly obvious when we consider that seventy-five percent of the general population has been estimated to be sensing types.[13] As the egalitarian movement emphasizes greater access to higher education, the college population will begin to reflect the makeup of the general population. From the data discussed above, we might hypothesize that scores on college entrance examinations are falling not because of a decline in students' native intelligence, but because of the greater numbers of sensing students who are taking these tests.

It becomes obvious, then, that there is a "new" student in the college classrooms, not only at Mercer but across the nation. There have always been some students like these, but they have been in the minority. Problems can occur in the college classroom when the New Students, now a majority, face the "old" faculty. A great deal of potential for disappointment and disillusionment exists on both sides.

Liberal Arts Faculty and New Students

Liberal arts faculty are often bewildered by and frustrated with the students they see in the classrooms of 1980. Unfamiliar with many of the new characteristics, faculty see New Students as hopelessly unprepared, or less bright, or less motivated than previous generations of students. The reasons are not hard to discover. L. Lee Knefelkamp puts it very well:

> Whatever our own socioeconomic background, most of us who are faculty were in the upper one-third of academic ability; we liked the vicarious tasks of learning; we liked them so much we never left the campus.

---

[12]Isabel Briggs Myers, *Gifts Differing* (Palo Alto, CA: Consulting Psychologists Press, 1980), p. 151.

[13]Lawrence, p. 24.

Indeed, learning became at once a means to achieving our vocational goals and our vocation itself. The classroom environments we create are rewarding to us and to students like us, but are often sources of great punishment and frustration for the "new students." They, in turn, are sources of frustration and challenge for us. We love our subject matter and want them to love it too—for the pure pleasure of exercising their minds. We want to be good teachers and feel a deep sense of pain when we don't "succeed." Clearly this problem can also be true of more traditional students. In either case, the classroom can be reduced to an environment of enormous threat to the sense of self of both the student and the faculty member.[14]

We have already discussed the students' "sense of self" as it relates to the educational experience; their views about the purposes of education and their clear preferences for certain types of activities can serve as a description of who they are, at least in their role as students.

If faculty members were to take a similar instrument as the students, what would they rate as highly important? Perhaps their scores on expectations for education would look opposite to their students' in many ways. New Students want practical, job-related training; most faculty would prefer that they encounter liberal learning as a way of broadening their options, not narrowing them to one job. Students expect a great deal of personal attention and support; faculty may feel that sharing their knowledge and views about their subject matter is the most personal relationship imaginable—they don't need or want to be "friends." New Students expect and need academic support services and special assistance; faculty view "remedial" programs with dismay and feel that students should be capable of learning on their own. Students want career advice largely related to earning the highest salaries in secure positions; faculty are keenly, painfully aware that their own career choices mean declining compensations and loss of security in the foreseeable future.

Not only would we project opposing expectations about what

---

[14]L. Lee Knefelkamp, "Faculty and Student Development in the 80's: Renewing the Community of Scholars," in Integrating Adult Development theory with Higher Education Practice, *Current Issues n Higher Education* 2:5 (1 October 1980): 15-16.

college is all about, but we would also predict that the faculty's preferred learning styles are very different from the New Students'. Liberal arts faculty would probably score high on the intuitive scale if they were to take the Myers-Briggs Type Indicator. Research by Isabel Briggs Myers shows that National Merit Finalists are more than eighty percent intuitives; Rhodes Scholars, ninety-three percent intuitives. By contrast, students in the Wharton School of Finance and Commerce were seventy-two percent sensors.[15]

In another study, faculty were asked to rate their students according to a variety of descriptions associated with student characteristics. Faculty consistently assigned the following descriptors to intuitive students: depth and originality of thought, imagination, ability to analyze, grasp of abstract ideas, and independence.[16] The study of the humanities, especially, requires these intuitive skills.[17] Small wonder that liberal arts faculty feel that the predominantly sensing students are different from themselves.

These differences may be one of the causes of low morale, a sense of discouragement, and tendencies toward despair that can be heard across the country whenever faculty gather to discuss their roles as teachers. Faculty have chosen their careers, as Knefelkamp says, for the love of learning rather than for the extrinsic rewards. How can they cope with students who do not recognize the same love? Must they resign themselves not only to declining compensations but also to the loss of the joy in learning and teaching? One liberal arts faculty member recently commented that his senior students were like chipmunks or squirrels, storing away separate little chunks of knowledge; they had no idea why they gathered these nuggets and no understanding of how they relate to each other. The faculty member asked, "Must I resign myself to these nugget-gatherers all the rest of my professional life? Do I have to give up the goals, aspirations, and joys that made me choose teaching?"

---

[15]Myers, *Gifts*, pp. 37-48.

[16]Ross, "Progress Report," p. 51.

[17]James E. Dunning, *Values and Humanities Study: An Operational Analysis of the Humanities Using the Myers-Briggs Type Indicator*, unpublished dissertation, Claremont Graduate School and University Center, 1970.

Seeing Ahead By Looking Back

From the faculty's point of view, the future with New Students may look pretty bleak. Perhaps what we need is some distance on the problem, a wider perspective. We have been focusing on the New Students and the faculty; now let us look at the tradition of the liberal arts. Perhaps we can find some common ground that faculty and students can share, and that they can build upon for the 1980s and beyond.

The study of liberal arts is presently regarded as the most impractical of all studies. Students report that their parents are unhappy with majors in philosophy, English, or history. "But what are you going to *do* with that education?" they ask. Liberal arts began, of course, as an "obsessively practical" course of study; David Halliburton quotes O. B. Hardison, Jr., on the inventors of the liberal arts curriculum:

> They attacked medieval culture for being impractical, and they wanted to reform society (through) their educational system. . . . They required mastery of Greek and Latin because in the fifteenth and sixteenth centuries most of the knowledge they considered essential—especially knowledge of eloquence—was found in the classics. They wrote in Latin because Latin was an international language.[18]

This practicality, Halliburton goes on to say, had as its base the most utilitarian of purposes—"concrete training":

> The humanists stressed rhetoric because it trained people to speak effectively. Their goal was to create an intellectual elite from which the state would draw its magistrates, its governors, its juries, its parliamentarians, and its educators.[19]

One of the most eloquent spokesmen for liberal education, and one of the most widely accepted, is John Henry Cardinal Newman. His essay "The Idea of a University" reminds us that liberal learning "is the

---

[18]Arthur W. Chickering et al., *Developing the College Curriculum: A Handbook for Faculty and Administrators* (Washington, DC: Council for the Advancement of Small Colleges, 1977), pp. 48-49.

[19]Ibid., p. 49.

great ordinary means to a great but ordinary end," and that "its end is fitness for the world":

> It is the education which gives a man a clear conscious view of his own opinions and judgments, a truth in developing them, an eloquence in expressing them, and a force in urging them. It teaches him to see things as they are, to go right to the point, to disentangle a skein of thought, to detect what is sophistical, and to discard what is irrelevant. It prepares him to fill any post with credit, and to master any subject with facility. It shows him how to accommodate himself to others, how to throw himself into their state of mind, how to bring before them his own, how to influence them, how to come to an understanding with them, how to bear with them. He is at home in any society, he has common ground with every class; he knows when to speak and when to be silent; he is able to converse, he is able to listen; he can ask a question pertinently, and gain a lesson seasonably, when he has nothing to impart himself; he is ever ready, yet never in the way; he is a pleasant companion, and a comrade you can depend upon; he knows when to be serious and when to trifle, and he has a sure tact which enables him to trifle with gracefulness and to be serious with effect. He has the repose of a mind which lives in itself, while it lives in the world, and which has resources for its happiness at home when it cannot go abroad.[20]

Most liberal arts faculty would probably agree with Newman's statement. But what about the New Students—could they accept these goals for their educational experience? Arthur Chickering suggests that if we translate Newman's words into educational goals, then perhaps we can begin to see some common ground.

---

[20]John Henry Cardinal Newman, "The Idea of a University," in *The Norton Anthology of English Literature*, ed. M.H.Abrams et al., 4th ed. New York: W. W. Norton, 1979), 2:1035-36.

Newman	Dimensions of Adult Development
1. "A clear conscious view of his own opinions and judgments, a truth in developing them, an eloquence in expressing them, and a force in urging them"	1. Ethical development, integrity
2. "To see things as they are, to go right to the point, to disentangle a skein of thought, to detect what is sophistical, and to discard what is irrelevant"	2. Critical thinking skills (analysis, synthesis, evaluation)
3. "To fill any post with credit, and to master any subject with facility"	3. Professional or vocational development
4. "He is at home in any society, he has common ground with every class"	4. Recognition of interdependence, humanitarian concern
5. "How to accommodate himself to others, . . . throw himself into their state of mind,. . . bring before them his own,. . . come to an understanding, . . . bear with them"	5. Interpersonal competence, empathy, understanding, cooperation with others
6. "A pleasant companion, and a comrade you can depend upon"	6. Capacity for intimacy
7. "Repose of mind which lives in itself, while it lives in the world"	7. Sense of identity[21]

[21]Arthur W. Chickering, "Adult Development: A Workable Vision for Higher Education" in "Integrating Adult Development Theory with Higher Education Practice," *Current Issues in Higher Education* 2:5 (1 October 1980): 2.

If we agree with Newman on the broad basis of liberal education, then we must acknowledge the legitimacy of such student concerns as professional/vocational development, values education, and interpersonal skills. We must, in fact, return to the ideal of educating the "whole person," an ideal which has received much lip service and very little honest acceptance.

There are many thorny issues attendant upon the decision to affirm the view of liberal arts in such areas as interpersonal skills, extracurricular programs, and vocational education—far too many to discuss fully here. Let us focus on just two of the dimensions Chickering describes—ethical development and critical thinking skills—and suggest some theoretical perspectives that might increase the probability that faculty and students will both benefit.

Bridging the Gap

Faculty have long advocated the study of liberal arts because they believe that such study produces people capable of critical thinking and grounded in ethical values. In other words, the common belief has been that students learn and develop by exposure—that the *content* is all-important. When we consider the substance of critical thinking and ethical values, though, we realize that changes take place inside the individual. If development is to occur at all, the individual learner must have a significant encounter with ideas that produce growth. What happens when the learner is not on the same "wave length" as the teacher? Obviously, possibilities for growth are diminished. If faculty believe that *what* they are teaching has real value, then they must also be aware that *how* they are presenting it, and *to whom*, is of great significance.

Faculty have been accustomed to a traditional learning process wherein one who knows (the teacher) presents ideas to one who does not (the student). The process has been described often as a kind of "filling up" where the knowledge in one container is poured into another. But even those of us who prospered under the traditional system of lecture realize that we did not merely open our ears and record—that there was a significant interaction going on inside our heads. Learning resulted not from the content per se, but from the interaction of the content with a perceiver ready to respond, to question, to revise, or to reject. The goal of an effective teacher is to set up clear channels so that the learning process can be facilitated. This goal requires that we understand both the process and the individual learner's response to it.

Most faculty would identify the learning process as having three essential components: acquisition of skills, mastery of content, and increased understanding of the complex issues in the field. If there is one notion that liberal arts faculty especially value, it is the last one; cognitive complexity can almost be equated with intellectual development. True knowledge in any field involves movement from simple understanding toward complexity in understanding.

Cognitive developmental theorists focus on this complexity as a framework for understanding the learning process in adults. According to these theorists, adult learners go through an irreversible sequence of stages as they progress along a knowledge continuum. Each stage is qualitatively different, not only in what is known but also in the value of the knowledge. Movement occurs from a simple, absolute view of truth toward a complex, pluralistic perspective. This concept is easy to relate to our own roles as learners. If we recall the knowledge we held as freshmen and compare it to the knowledge we hold as professionals in our respective fields, we can see the increase in cognitive development as well as in skills and content mastery.

There is often a basic mismatch, however, between faculty expectations and the level of cognitive development in students. Teachers are well aware that their content mastery and skills level are far above the students', but they often forget that the way they view knowledge— the structure of their thoughts—is highly complex. Listen to the voice of a student commenting on tests, and the voice of a teacher who makes the tests:

> *Student:*
> "I have a fear of tests. I don't know what I'm supposed to know. Teachers say, 'You should have gotten this from what I told you there.' Teachers should teach what they know. Sometimes when you ask a question, teachers will answer you, but they won't really tell you. A good teacher is one who tells you what you're supposed to know."
>
> *Teacher:*
> "In exams, there are questions I've asked where I can think up three or four possible answers. It tends to

upset students because they feel there should be one;
. . . there aren't nice clear answers for the vast majority
of situations."[22]

What we hear in these voices is familiar. Students feel there is one right answer and the authority figure's role is to hand it over. Teachers perceive the complexity of the subject and expect students to see it, too.

This mismatch is the reason for teaching, of course. If all people perceived subjects in the same way, we could do without teachers. What is needed, however, is what Clyde A. Parker refers to as an "optimal mismatch." In a consulting project with teachers, Parker found that

> the faculty were expecting students to deal with information, data, and knowledge in the ways that Perry described some of the more mature Harvard seniors, but we found . . . that most students were not prepared to recognize the contextual and relativistic nature of knowledge, let alone to take personal responsibility for all their decisions or commitments; they were, to use Perry's labels, "dualists." That is, they looked to the faculty for *the* correct answers.[23]

Parker tried to provide this "optimal mismatch" by having teachers realize the level their students were on, then gradually bring them along—"stretch" them, as Parker put it—toward more complex levels of intellectual functioning.

A significant amount of work is being done on applying cognitive development theory to instructional design. One particular model that is easy to grasp and has clear concepts we can relate to teaching is William Perry's conceptualization, *Forms of Intellectual and Ethical Development in the College Years: A Scheme*.[24] Perry's original model suggested nine positions along a complexity scale, but those who have

---

[22]D. Froberg and Clyde A. Parker, *Progress Report on the Developmental Instruction Project,* unpublished manuscript (University of Minnesota, 1976), pp. 23, 17.

[23]Clyde A. Parker and Jane Lawson, "From Theory to Practice to Theory: Consulting with College Faculty," *Personnel and Guidance Journal* 56 (1978): 424.

[24]Cambridge, MA: Harvard University Press, 1970.

worked extensively with the model (Parker and others) have refined it to four positions.

Dualism—"The learner views himself as a receptacle ready to receive truth; as a result, he has difficulty with academic tasks requiring recognition of conflicting points of view or even use of his own opinion." Issues are seen as either black or white, no grey; the teacher is the authority, the one with the answers.

Multiplicity—Learner sees more diversity or plurality in the ways of considering the subject. "This plurality is perceived as an aggregate of factors without internal structure or external relations. Thus, anyone has a right to his own opinion. No criteria have yet been established to evaluate the merits of one opinion against another. . . ." (Example) "Things can be a hundred different ways. Both sides can bring in a ton of evidence to support their views. Both are equally right. Everybody is right. That's disillusioning."

Relativism—Knowledge is seen as even more complex, with differing contextual frames. Students are able to analyze, compare, evaluate. (Example) "There are so many ways of looking at it. It depends upon many factors . . . I try to keep flexibility in my conclusions . . ."

Commitment in Relativism—Student still perceives all the contextual complexity, but begins to form personal identity by making choices. "Commitment refers to the integrative, affirmative function of choosing among alternatives on the basis of prechosen criteria and values."[25]

Study of the progress of adult development suggests that most undergraduates, especially freshmen and sophomores, will fall within the dualistic positions; only graduate students begin to approach the higher levels of relativism.[26] The Perry model can begin to make clear

---

[25] Condensed and abstracted from L. Lee Knefelkamp and Cornfeld, "Combining Student Stage and Style in the Design of Learning Environments," and Clyde A. Parker and Jane M. Lawson, "Individualized Approach to Improving Instruction," reproduced in *Selected Papers* (see note 3), pp. 27-43.

[26] Parker and Lawson, *Selected Papers*, pp. 20-21.

how faculty members' distance from their students in cognitive complexity can be a significant factor in the learning process.

A recent study at Ohio State University compared ratings on the Perry scheme with scores on the Myers-Briggs. Sensors were found to be primarily dualists, while intuitives were primarily multiplistic.[27] When we add information about preferred learning styles to the measures of cognitive complexity, we can see how New Students prefer highly structured, clear-cut learning tasks; immediate concrete knowledge rather than abstract theory; and direct answers from an authority figure. They seem to be operating on the lower end of the complexity scale. Perhaps we should regard New Students as immature learners, not as inferior learners. This view removes the pejorative label and replaces it with one that is more positive and accepting.

Regardless of where students are on the cognitive developmental continuum, they all feel a certain amount of risk in the learning process. Such a commonality suggests that there may be certain dimensions which will be useful to all learners. One such dimension is what Nevitt Sanford calls "challenge and support." Sanford proposes that all students can meet great challenges intellectually or personally, provided that they also receive appropriate degrees of support. In an environment with too much challenge, students may feel overwhelmed and retreat or deny the experience. Too much support, however, can restrict learning as well. Students may report high satisfaction but demonstrate little or no growth. The best learning environment, according to Sanford, appears to be one where challenge is balanced with support.[28]

These four factors affect the degree of challenge and support in the learning environment:

1. The type of assignment/experience—Clearly an essay exam requiring highly complex thought is a greater challenge than a multiple-choice exam that requires only recognition.
2. The degree of structure—Students who want detailed syllabi, point-by-point enumeration of grading practices, or specific

---

[27]Robert F. Rodgers, unpublished research (Columbus, OH: Ohio State University).

[28]Nevitt Sanford in *Search for Relevance*, ed. Joseph Axelrod et al. (San Francisco, CA: Jossey-Bass Inc., 1969), p. 17.

page-length assignments are asking for a high degree of structure in their learning situation.

3. The amount of diversity—For students unable to make clear choices, a great amount of diversity in assignments, points of view, and alternatives can create a high-challenge learning environment.

4. The degree of personalism—The coolly rational, distant professor standing before a class of several hundred students presents an impersonal learning situation, a high challenge for some students.

What students perceive as challenging and what they view as supportive changes according to individual learning preferences and level of maturity. For example, college professors would probably dislike a learning situation where every moment was scheduled, every activity detailed, every new topic clearly defined. For a less mature learner, this attention to structure might be perceived as support, while the more mature learner could find it a great challenge just to endure such regimentation.

We must remember that each time a learner goes into a new situation, the process starts all over again. A Ph.D. in history may prove to be a desperate dualist as a new homeowner, seeking out "authorities" for "the answer" to such unfamiliar problems as broken faucets and faulty switches.

Individualizing the Learning Process for New Students

After reviewing several basic ideas about how students learn, let us turn to the specific topic at hand: how liberal arts faculty can help New Students master the challenge of college learning tasks. The goals are easy to state, if hard to achieve: faculty want students to master skills and content, and they want students to move into more complex cognitive developmental processes.

Methods for achieving these goals are suggested by the data available on New Students plus the four factors of assignment type, structure, diversity, and personalism. For example, we have seen that New Students prefer concrete learning experiences on which they can build toward abstract understanding. Assignments can be structured to present experience earlier, theory later. Examples of various plans to implement this approach can be seen in a volume published at the

University of Nebraska-Lincoln (1978) called "Multidisciplinary Piagetian-Based Programs for College Freshmen." In subject areas such as English where "hands-on" learning seems less appropriate, models may help to illustrate how assignments may be done.

The amount of structure needed by New Students appears to be quite high. They gain confidence (support) to attempt the challenge of learning by knowing precisely what is required of them and when. They prefer sequential learning tasks, building a linear concept rather than having a global concept presented all at once. Open-ended assignments, independent projects, or self-designed learning situations seem to be extremely challenging to New Students. Too much diversity in ideas, classroom environment, or assignments can cause anxiety.

Finally, we recall that New Students prefer a higher degree of personalism than traditional students. Because they are unsure of themselves, they want a great deal of feedback from their teachers, staff members, and peers. New Students may adapt quite well to group activities and collaborative learning. In some English classrooms at Mercer, for example, peer evaluation of writing seems to meet some of the needs for interpersonal contact, immediate feedback, and clarifying objectives. Students are uneasy at first when asked to respond to a colleague's paper ("How do I know? You're the teacher!"), but they rapidly move toward greater confidence as they see how the peer review system operates.

Looking at assignments, classroom methods, and tests according to how well they match up with the way students learn can be an effective learning process. Not only does such study help us to see whether the goals have been achieved, but it also helps us to analyze our assumptions. Knefelkamp and Cornfeld's work with the learning process disclosed that:

> we frequently had asked students to demonstrate competencies at a complexity level that was either too high or for what they had not rehearsed; and that we designed most of our learning options to fit our own typologies and thus omitted options that matched with students of different typologies.[29]

---

[29]Knefelkamp and Cornfeld, *Selected Papers*, p. 31.

If faculty can expand the repertoire of teaching techniques open to them, perhaps they can greatly increase both their own satisfaction and their students' learning. We do not mean to suggest that every teacher treat each student differently, designing thirty or forty plans for instruction for a single class. What we are suggesting is that an overall understanding of how students learn and where they are in the process can help faculty to meet the needs of students who sit in the classrooms before them. No suggestion could be more in line with the liberal arts philosophy, for it asks that students be regarded as individuals with unique and identifiable characteristics. Furthermore, this suggestion recognizes the college's moral and ethical commitment to teaching: we must not only open the doors of our institutions, but we must also do our part to help students to learn.

Institutionalizing the Commitment to Teaching and Learning

Most faculty members have spent years learning how to be good students and how to master the knowledge in their area of specialization. They are understandably chagrined to find that their students may not be interested in learning the same things in the same way. Often faculty get conflicting messages from their institutions about the value of teaching: while administrative officers espouse the value of teaching, they often reward other professional duties. Little attention has been devoted to teaching in the liberal arts college. As colleges begin to compete on ever fiercer levels, however, good teaching will become a significant factor in institutional survival. Colleges cannot afford to ignore it any longer.

If teaching and learning are to be truly significant, an institution must affirm and promote teachers' efforts to learn more about who their students are, how they learn, and how they may be taught. Colleges will need to provide faculty development funds, to sponsor research in learning, to devise means whereby new ideas can be shared, and to go far beyond the traditional "aggressive neglect" of teaching. Borland describes "aggressive neglect" as the destructive stance wherein an institution espouses the value of teaching, but does not reward it with faculty development funds, promotion, tenure, or compensation.[30] With proper institutional support, faculty will be willing and able to meet the challenges ahead.

---

[30]David Borland "Aggressive Neglect, Matrix Organization, and Student Development," *Journal of College Student Personnel* 18 (1977): 35-39.

Long-Range Implications

We have suggested throughout this essay that the influx of New Students into liberal arts colleges can be seen not as a threat, but as a challenge. What may be projected as long-range results if colleges rise to this challenge?

First, and most selfishly, those colleges who can meet the challenges will survive, while those who deny it may well sink. But beyond this immediate benefit lie some very worthy goals. The liberal arts can perhaps fulfill its promise of a better society of well-rounded, competent citizens. If we believe in the worth of each individual, then we must surely welcome the egalitarian movement in higher education. New Students can serve to test our liberality and faith in an open society.

On a more personal level, faculty and students may begin to regard each other as partners in the educational endeavor. It's true that faculty, staff, and administrators have a great deal to teach New Students; but they can help us to learn, too. Mina Shaughnessy, an English professor at the City University of New York, completed before her death one of the most significant books ever to be written about writing. *Errors and Expectations* chronicles not only her research into student work, but also her growing awareness of the New Students she was working with:

> From these students we have also begun to learn much about learning and teaching. Capable because of their maturity of observing the processes they are going through as learners, they can alert us easily and swiftly to the effects of instruction. They work, in this sense, collaboratively with teachers in ways that are impossible with child learners. In a hurry, also, to learn what we have to teach them, they press us to discover the most efficient ways of presenting what we would have them understand.
>
> Once he grants students the intelligence and will they need to master what is being taught, the teacher begins to look at his students' difficulties in a more fruitful way: he begins to search in what students write and say for clues to their reasoning and their purposes, and in what *he* does for gaps and misjudgments. He begins

teaching anew.[31]

Liberal learning is as valuable to our society now as it has ever been. As faculty adapt to the needs of different student populations, they become part of the tradition preserving liberal learning, at the same time demonstrating the ability of liberally educated individuals to accept the challenge of change.

[31]Mina Shaughnessy, *Errors and Expectations* (New York: Oxford University Press, 1977), pp. 291-92.

Viva the Liberal Arts!
Viva Specialization!

Edwin Harwood

Experts and Amateurs

An enduring complaint of the American higher educational system ten to fifteen years ago was that we were producing too many specialist technicians and not enough generalists. We were educating too many of our students in the narrow ways of professional careers to the neglect of the whole man or woman which it was the special province of liberal arts education to foster. Now, with a faltering economy and shortages of oil along with deficits of petroleum engineers, solar energy physicists, and other technical specialists very much in demand, one hears fewer complaints about the overproduction of narrowly specialized technical workers and rather more complaints about the overabundance of liberal arts graduates who find a knowledge of Milton or Shakespeare quite unnecessary for driving a cab.

It was certainly a fallacy back then to assume, as too many did, that specialization and the liberal arts were somehow antagonistic. One cannot turn engineers loose on society who have had only a smattering of engineering courses along with everything else. Yet the same can also be said for the student in English, History, or any other field who hopes to become accomplished in his chosen field of study. While students of the latter fields may not require as many specialized courses as the engineer, only a detailed command of the facts and generalizations in a subject gives the scholar—whether student or teacher—the ability to achieve fresh judgments in a field.

At the same time, I feel the university must encourage amateur intellectual involvements that fall outside a chosen branch of study. I take this to be a major dilemma of higher education in America, which the liberal arts curriculum was meant to overcome. But can a liberal arts curriculum achieve the goal of humanistic training without a corresponding liberal arts ethic? The thoughts in this essay address that problem: how to create the ethic that will allow the university to merge specialized training with amateur pursuits.

Too many of us—students and professors alike—suffer from a stern specialization. We behave like seventeenth century Puritans ready and willing to serve the New Model Army of our chosen guild but scornful of the amateurism that brought the cavaliers of Charles I to ruin. I recall an incident that amused me while I was a graduate student at the University of Chicago in the early 1960s. Several graduate students in my department gave wide circulation to the report of one who said he had "caught" a noted demographer reading Karl Marx's *Das Kapital* in his office during work hours. This professor was hardly interested in radical sociology, which hadn't yet become the fashion it was to become five years later. What puzzled us was how a man who researched the problem of fertility control so tirelessly could find time to read an old economics classic.

We assumed that a scholar was known only by his "colors of specialization." And as students we were in the habit of referring to a professor as a "small groups man" or "a collective behavior man" or "a race relations man." It is true that some quite distinguished sociologists had risen above such designations. There were scholars such as Edward A. Shils, Robert Nisbet, and George C. Homans who happened to be, as it appeared, in sociology for administrative reasons of convenience. They wrote on problems that defied compartmentalization and often contributed to journals outside their discipline. This distinction between the generalist-scholar and the professional lingers on in sociology because there was a time when a broad investigation of society and history was what social scientists mainly concerned themselves with. The increased specialization and progressive narrowing of research interests and techniques, however, have drastically reduced the ranks of the former in favor of the technically proficient "professional." One consequence of this bifurcation is that tension between the specialist and generalist (gentleman-scholar) persists to the detriment of the community of scholars. It affects students and professors alike, both of whom may end their amateur intellectual involvements with their undergraduate work. Indeed, so great is the pressure to stay close to some corner of a field whose contours are warmly familiar that even leisure reading may become burdened with professional purposes. Thus I recall how, when I first began teaching in the mid-60s, a student had written a lively paper on the angry English novelists and playwrights of the 1950s for a course of mine on Industrial Society. I was intrigued by the novels he cited and decided to follow up on his sources a year later. To legitimate my grant of time to this, I took notes of sociological relevance on each novel, which prompted my wife to ask if I could ever read anything just for the pleasure of it.

To resolve the conflict between the "two cultures" of intense specialization and amateur scholarly involvement we must educate not amateurs or experts but rather individuals who can move with some ease between both positions and who, when they work outside their field, can do so with good conscience and good craftsmanship. Granted, we cannot work as amateurs in *every* field or even most, but we should be able to step comfortably from, say, sociology into literature, or chemistry into biology.

The Fashionable Bias

America's technological superiority, though now challenged by the Japanese and Europeans, rests heavily on the vocational specialization offered by her universities and institutes. Surely this must be counted a gain not for America alone but for many societies that have benefited from the exports of our technological culture, from agricultural implements to silicon chips. But much more than improved living standards around the world is at stake. We must be concerned with those improvements in the quality of life that go beyond the crude indicator of the GNP. What kinds of goods and services do we want? Once we have settled priorities of expenditure through a mixture of public and private market decisions, technician-specialists will assume the task of translating public will into tangible reality. Our high standard of living, which rests on the rather mundane foundations of skilled specialists of all kinds, from tool and die makers to computer software designers, is the sine qua non for the involvement of large numbers of people in humanistic pursuits since only an affluent society can make available the leisure for such activities.

Surely we are grateful to specialists like Bach and Bartok for choosing a rather narrow course of occupational training, though I am not sure whether it was through the active promotion of an enlightened few or the technological innovations in the recording industries that brought about their well-deserved recognition among a wider public. The economy achieved in the production of vinyl-acetate long-playing records brought incredibly esoteric musical compositions to publics that would have had no opportunity to hear such music forty to fifty years ago. This was an achievement of narrow technicians with vision. I have to remind students who relish the now fashionable talk about technological depersonalization that some in society must do dull jobs in a factory if the highbrow commodities students enjoy—the $5.98 LP record or $5.95 paperback classic—is to be available at a price they can afford. H. S. Bennett informs us in his *The Pastons and Their England* that Oxford students sometimes pledged garments or books when they lacked ready cash for tuition fees. That was over 400 years ago. Books, like family plate, were our equivalent of gilt-edged securities, and we have a hard time appreciating the cash value of books to people in an age that was both considerably less affluent and more materialistic than our own. (Bennett also reminds us of how common it was for fathers to improve a shaky financial position by pledging their daughters in marriage.)

Those who argue in favor of a broadly humanistic curriculum are right to point out that technology is not applied *in vacuo* and that consequently moral and political priorities are crucial. These will be decided in part by the value commitments college graduates take with them into the institutions of work and professional life, and into the communities they enter. Sensitivity to social problems and the ability to exercise mature judgment in setting moral priorities demand the broader reach of the humanities. So do other sensibilities that, under the pressure of bureaucratic busyness and the scramble for careers, seem to be on the verge of extinction: easy-going sociability and the ability to take an interest in things and people that have no relation to the "pay-off matrix" of the career.[1]

Though we need to leaven the vocational training of specialists with a good liberal arts program—and, as stressed earlier, with a liberal arts ethic—we should not undermine the morale of specialists by assaulting their subject matter and their choice of a narrow vocation. Building the fuel-efficient auto or an economical solar heating system will require the know-how of highly specialized engineers. Those who wish to have such talents must undergo a prolonged period of training. If we hope to limit uncontrolled population growth, we must call upon medical researchers, demographers, survey researchers, people like my professor at Chicago caught reading out of his field, and others who have concentrated years of study on how modern practices of fertility control can be communicated to traditional peoples. One hopes desperately that these specialists are wholeheartedly engaged in the narrow course of action for as long as it takes to do the job. I cannot imagine, for example, how the radical graduate students of sociology (thankfully more numerous eight to ten years ago than now) will ever find in Marxist-Leninist "praxis" answers to the problems of pollution, energy, or hunger. Mostly such ideological fare serves, if taken seriously, as an opiate to mask disenchantment with the discipline demanded by technical study. It becomes a shoddy substitute for the careful and objective scholarship that is really useful to society.

If specialization is a gain for society through improving technology, it is also true of university scholarship in every field. Though much that is trivial goes on because of excessive specialization, most would have to agree that our knowledge of any subject is improved because our best scholars on one or several occasions in their career decided on a narrow course of research. It occurs to me that the noted historian, John U. Nef, could not have convinced us to think freshly on the beginnings of the industrial revolution had he not chosen first to study the British coal industry in great detail. His detailed investigation of the coal industry in the seventeenth century showed that the

---

[1]David Riesman examines the erosion of sociability in his "Notes on Meritocracy," *Daedalus* (Summer 1967): 899.

important developments in large-scale capitalist enterprise had been underway at least two centuries before the rise of the factory system in the late eighteenth century. He brought to light other important findings which threw into doubt most everything that that great generalist Max Weber had to say on the subject of the evolution of industrial capitalism in the West.[2]

So, viva specialization! But with a caution.

Unguided by any higher principle of organization or relevance, specialization can become degenerative. In universities it can lead to trivial research of the sort that wastes time and talent and may impose other hidden costs to the community of scholars (some of which I shall discuss later). Many journals have become the litter bins of research that is trivial, shallow, and really little more than "make work" for careerist motives.

Degenerate specialization has its counterpart in the kind of anti-intellectualism that masqueraded as humanistic commitment ten to fifteen years ago on many campuses. Civil and balanced skepticism gave way to political and moral cynicism as the concern for crusades—some tinged with a bizarre yearning for totalitarian politics—captured a large constituency on campus. All this shows, I think, that some educators were failing their job. The student who seriously intended to do something about the world's problems would hardly profit from reading Herbert Marcuse. Undergraduate interest in the burgeoning works by authors seeking to cash in on the market for alienation showed how a kind of underground scholarship had evolved which linked the disaffected young to the jaded and cynical old. This was degenerate humanism and was as much a peril to a balanced liberal arts education as degenerate specialization.

When we debunk the narrow engineering curriculum or any other line of vocational specialization we risk our own and other societies' future well-being. Too much applause and encouragement of the humanities in our best universities might tempt students to abandon vocational specialization, particularly in fields like engineering which require more self-discipline and concentration than some others. Requirements in the humanities majors are sometimes less rigorous. Possibly they are more fun. Too many defections by students who have

---

[2]John U. Nef, *The Cultural Foundations of Industrial Civilization* (Cambridge: The University Press, 1958), and other of his works.

been told that it is more noble to discover themselves and explore life's meaning—which the liberal arts bias can encourage—will limit the capacity of Western society to meet the pressing demands imposed by scarce resources, overpopulation, and so forth. I feel this is less of a problem today than ten years ago, in part because of the changed economic environment and the consequent devaluation of the generalist's skills. Those who were shouting for "relevance" ten years ago now quietly ply their trades as security analysts, accountants, insurance salesmen, and so forth.

Striking the Balance

Vocationalism should not be incompatible with the liberal arts goal of the university. Most universities round out engineering curricula with required courses in the humanities and social sciences. But the content of courses for nonmajors might be better adapted to the postgraduate concerns of nonmajors by greater sensitivity to the kinds of issues that would appeal to them as well as to the majors who are specializing in a discipline. Readings could be selected, for example, on the basis of their intrinsic intellectual appeal and manner of exposition and less in terms of a narrow disciplinary classification. The teacher thus might spark the kind of enthusiasm in students that would carry interest in the subject beyond the course's end.

Thus students preparing for careers in business and engineering might retain more from a course on modern society that included articles in *Fortune*, the *Atlantic Monthly* or *Saturday Review* wherein discussions of social and economic problems are more accessible than the technical social science journals. The latter too frequently communicate technical disciplinary issues over how best to employ such-and-such a concept in a research area, or what method to use, and so forth. Scholars who write for college-educated people rather than just their colleagues should be called to service in undergraduate courses.

This does not mean that all courses should be watered down. A well-taught specialized course can be very exciting and introduce the student to readings he would never choose for himself. A course in small groups or social psychology cannot without substantial loss avoid specialized research and terminology. On the other hand a course on industrial society would get more across to students by steering clear of the professional journals in favor of authors who write in an exciting idiom. A course on social movements or collective behavior would stick with students if lectures and readings presented lively histories and contemporary case studies of such, saving the conceptual baggage, the theory, and those "reformulations of concepts" that are the small change of scholarly exchange for the last two weeks of the semester.[3]

What Ails Undergraduate Teaching?

Liberal arts students must learn to reason clearly and write well; the assimilation of facts and generalizations is secondary to this goal. It is no secret that many of us merely *scan* our professional journals. When we read for pleasure, we go elsewhere. And even professional monographs are more likely to be read in their entirety if well written. Good writing sparks enthusiasm for a subject and this is absolutely vital for students who do not yet have the scholar's motive for putting up with dull stuff. All other things being equal, the scholar who thinks clearly and writes as though he actually enjoys the act of communicating should be preferred to the individual who, stranded somewhere along the tenure trail, felt he just had to "get something out" for the lucrative textbook market or who so dedicated himself to his research tasks that he never took the time to learn how to communicate knowledge in a lively way.

More attention needs to be given to student writing although, as things stand, faculty concern appears to end with the freshman year and, through collective ignorance, it is assumed that this is the exclusive job of an English department. Once I thought that students in English or History were advantaged in this regard. It is not so. I have not found English majors to be much better at writing than other majors.

On term papers, most teachers check to make sure that essential facts were stated, that some of the reasoning is at least logical, and that something original by way of conclusion gets expressed. Clumsy phrasing, redundancy, the use of too many prepositions to tack on extra thoughts as they come to mind, stale metaphors, and careless use of concepts are things which many teachers are either not competent to correct or do not have the time to correct. Thinking back on my

---

[3]Most of these examples are taken from sociology. Some disciplines—history, for example—may not have to strike the balance. Others—like psychology—are probably much in need of doing so.

undergraduate years, I can remember several English professors taking pains with my style. In other departments, teachers limited their effort to marginalia—"Are you sure of this?," "I wonder about that," "good point," "agree," and so forth—and then gave a summary verdict in two or three sentences at the end, beginning, "You might have considered. . . ." Students should receive more than this on at least some papers.

How does one explain our lack of interest in student papers? In part it derives from the professional socialization of the graduate schools. Good ideas and research disciplined by state-of-the-art technique count for much. The style and evocative interest of written material are secondary if they count at all. We scan student papers for their content in much the same way that we scan professional articles. We are taught in effect to consider our writing as intradisciplinary memoranda and very likely communicate this to students through the limited attention we give to term papers. Possibly we are afflicted with the notion that any paper or book which is pleasurable to read cannot be taken too seriously. It may not be "work" if it is fun.

The cursory treatment of student exposition also stems in part from that squeeze on time which has undermined concern for undergraduate education in general. Nevitt Sanford sums up the attitude of the postwar professoriat: "This would be a great place if it were not for the students."[4] Even when teachers do the course work that is required of them, the undergraduate teaching is still too often at or below and not above and beyond the call of duty. Here we see most clearly how the issue of liberal arts education cannot always be solved simply by changing the curriculum or starting a new experimental college or funding an experimental program in an established one. Real dedication to the time-consuming reading and grading of student work cannot be substituted for the rhetoric of innovation, new programs, and so forth; and there is also no substitute for meeting and talking with students in an unhurried and civilized manner, instead of treating them like clients in a dermatology clinic who have administrative or intellectual itches that need only five to ten minutes' diagnosis.

Esteem in the academic profession at many schools goes to those who keep abreast of their field, keep up with "the literature" as we say

---

[4]Nevitt Sanford, *Where Colleges Fail* (San Francisco: Jossey-Bass, Inc., 1967), p. 104.

(not facetiously either), and contribute more of the same which their colleagues then feel obliged to read. Teaching above and beyond the call of duty is not a stepping stone to career advancement. Exceptionally good teachers will be rewarded at the institutions where they teach, often with sizeable money prizes and a permit to stay on at their school which for some may be the equivalent of a lease on life. But this has no national repercussions. In what I call the "meritropolis," the large university towns and those institutes and industries coming within their orbit, a man's measure is determined not by those who know him intimately but by the extent to which he is known by many who have never met him and know him only through his creative productions.[5]

Some social distortion seems inevitable when men and women become too concerned with the professional pecking order to the neglect of other facets of personal life. Character and good morals were more important than intellect when colleges coupled religious training with education. Though we are glad to be free of this, perhaps we have gone too far. The *in loco parentis* function of universities has been attacked not just because standards of adolescent social conduct have been changing in our postbourgeois society but more because this function was narrowly couched in double-standard regulations that sought primarily to control *outward* behavior and to avoid "embarrassing situations." It could be called a negative program for maintaining an acceptable level of behavior rather than a positive program of character building of the kind that colleges at one time did try to achieve and the military academies, though to a lesser extent today, still do. Regulations are poor substitutes for the personal example provided by mature educators. In sum, the university is a moral community as well as an intellectual workshop.

Conclusion

The problem of liberal arts is not exclusively a problem of undergraduate education. It is also a problem for the educators. If they cannot find the time to wander afield, how can they convince undergraduates of the importance of a liberal arts program? To produce

---

[5]Eric Hoffer, author of *The True Believer* and a professional "local" with a cosmopolitan audience, asked on TV: "What is fame? Fame is when a lot of people you don't know know you. What good is that?"

research of value to scholars requires specialization. But I have argued that since some of this research is often valueless, the persons doing it might consider devoting some of their time to those subjects that did interest them even though they might never become experts or scholars in the area. Surely it is irrational for a scholar to spend all of his time reading in one or a few very narrow subfields because he feels compelled to keep up, when he could be reading good works in other fields and perhaps writing on topics of greater interest to him. When too much time is consumed in the reading of dull stuff the educator's boredom and tiredness eventually will be communicated to students who then realize that keeping up with the literature in some obscure subfield may be the price one pays for pursuing an academic career. In many fields today, keeping abreast of the literature is no longer possible—until a way is found to stretch the twenty-four-hour day beyond its present span.

In B. F. Skinner's utopia for postindustrial man, *Walden Two*, the skeptic weekend visitor professor Burris finds that the community's library, though small, had stocked all the works he had been wanting to read. What had he been reading back at his university whose library was surely much more adequately equipped? Mainly junk. He used detective stories for relaxation no doubt because such material had not, like serious literature, been defined as some other scholar's job. He thought he could indulge serious interests outside his own field only in a place like *Walden Two* which not only did not define all areas of knowledge as some specialist's job but warmly encouraged amateur interests.

One cannot divorce the issue of undergraduate education from the professional constraints that educators face in the meritropolis. Mere innovative revisions that tinker with the liberal arts program are not alone sufficient. Educators cannot convince students of the need for a broadly humanistic education if they are themselves so highly specialized that they lack time for learning what goes on in other fields.

An institutional mechanism for doing this might be an "exchange seminar." A professor in one field, say, history, might team up with another in political science or anthropology, sharing the course work of two seminars. It may be that a teacher of psychology, sociology, physics, or geology feels played out one semester or a year. Why couldn't he or she participate in a course taught in the humanities or social sciences? Some physical scientists are very interested in current social and political issues and might find participation in a political science or sociology course the very opportunity they need to merge their duty to students with their current extradisciplinary interest.

Emancipation from overspecialization should be our goal. As things stand today, many educators feel compelled to keep in step with a narrow subfield of a discipline, which leads them to labor too long over much that is tedious and trivial. The print explosion has advanced specialized knowledge and this on balance represents a gain to society and education. But it can distort the educational function of universities. More and more is being written about smaller fragments of the total human experience. Perhaps the real function of education is to teach students to learn to judge what they do not need to know, and how to discriminate quickly in their reading so that they can concentrate their time on the best and return to the librarian the books which seemed to serve someone's need to get along in his career rather than the enlightenment of men and women.

In conclusion, long live the liberal arts for their contribution to a humanistic culture! And long live specialization for providing us with the standard of living that makes it possible!

"Genuine" Liberal Education: An Excellent Preparation for Law School

Joseph E. Claxton

Altruism combined with realism; knowledge of fundamental principles and capacity to apply them; courage to insist on the right and patience to achieve it; understanding of the timidity of the weak; fearlessness of the domination of the powerful; sympathy for the mistakes of the indiscreet; caution of the craftiness of the unprincipled; enthusiasm for that which is fine and inspiring; reverence for that which is sacred; these are some of the attributes of great lawyers.

(Justin Miller,
Dean, 1930-1934
Duke University School of Law)

The Liberal Arts and Legal Education
Viewed from a Church-Related Institution

Any legal educator who seeks to analyze the value of a liberal arts background as preparation for law school ventures into dangerous waters. Few undergraduate-level faculty members are likely to be enthralled at the prospect of instruction in the worth of their endeavors by a representative of the sometimes mercenary world of the law. An educator whose intellectual and professional life hinges on the nuances of the Uniform Commercial Code may not be viewed as having either the philosophical insight or the moral sensibilities that, in a collective sense, should be inherent in any liberal arts faculty. It is possible to begin, however, on a very positive note. To the extent that a liberal arts education is intended to provide maximum opportunities for *disciplined* self-expression and self-fulfillment, there is a definite compatibility between a liberal education and a legal education. Indeed, a young person who emphasizes a balance of the humanities, arts, natural sciences, and social sciences—regardless of the person's specific area of concentration—has the opportunity to establish an intellectual framework of the sort that is essential for academic *and emotional* success in law school.

There is a clear identity of intellectual purpose between a liberal arts education and a subsequent legal education. Without firm substance to support it, of course, any statement of this sort deserves to be treated as empty rhetoric, reminiscent of the most callow college freshman. That firm substance is found in the fundamental aims of most educational institutions (aims that perhaps should be present, at least to some degree, in all educational institutions worthy of the name).

What are these aims of education that are so basic to both a liberal education and a legal education? They have been well articulated by Dr. R. Kirby Godsey, the President of Mercer University, in his mission statement for that school.[1] Mercer is a relatively small (5,000 students) university, and it is church-related (Baptist). Thus, it admittedly is outside the norm in an era of large, tax-supported "mega-universities." It is very similar to many other universities, however, in that, for most of its history it has had both a liberal arts and a law school component (and in recent years other divisions as well). In specifying the educational aims of Mercer as a university, therefore, any president would have to be aware (as Godsey expressly noted in his

---

[1]R. Kirby Godsey, "The Mission of Mercer University: A Blueprint for the Future," in *New Pathways: a Dialogue in Christian Higher Education,* ed. Ben C. Fisher (Macon, GA: Mercer University Press, 1980), pp. 9-16.

mission statement) that he was dealing with an institution that provides both a liberal and a professional education. That essential fact naturally helps push Mercer toward the sort of intellectual diversity that most institutions of higher education profess to desire. Moreover, Mercer's church-related character probably has broadened rather than limited its intellectual base in many ways. This is a trend that has been evident during the last quarter century in other, more widely known church-related schools, especially some that are affiliated with the Catholic Church. The educational aims set forth in Godsey's analysis are these:

1. To develop the ability to think more clearly and precisely.
2. To heighten the ability to use language more effectively.
3. To cultivate the ability to solve problems more effectively.
4. To enhance the students' ability to analyze data, to compare, and to extrapolate.
5. To increase the capacity for self-transcendence.
6. To enhance the ability to listen.
7. To enable a person to learn how to learn.
8. To enlarge the capacity for informed judgments and discriminating moral choices.
9. To understand the impact of religious commitments upon learning and work.
10. To contribute to the preservation, dissemination, and advancement of knowledge.

One may suspect that very few faculty members or students who have the opportunity to participate in the give-and-take of liberal arts education would dispute the legitimacy of most of these aims. Furthermore, all ten can have direct relevance not just to legal education in a university setting, but to the application of that education to "real-world" problems by experienced attorneys.

Candor compels the admission that a cynic could suggest that the capacity to make "discriminating moral choices" (item eight) and "to understand the impact of religious commitments upon learning and work" (item nine) are not inherent aims of legal education. To go one step more, it might be said that an understanding of the role of religious commitments ought to be accorded little attention even in liberal arts colleges, perhaps including those that are church-related. With due acknowledgment of the "paper chase" legend, however, I submit that the strongest moral choices can be reached by the finely honed intellectual processes that are so characteristic of a mind thoroughly trained in the law, and that a liberal arts background can and should provide a major element of the ethical framework within which those processes operate. As for the impact of religious commitments upon learning and work, it is not necessary for either a liberal educator or a legal educator to subscribe to a certain set of religious views in order to accept Godsey's explanation that "the development of belief and ultimate religious perspectives remains very much a part of making decisions about one's life and work."[2] The impact of religious commitments is not just a matter for historical examination. When accorded in a proper way, attention to the present impact of those commitments in an educational institution need not (and to insure the strength of the institution must not) be threatening to those persons in the academic community who do not share the institution's religious orientation. Even in the law school world of torts and contracts it is still possible to fulfill Godsey's vision of "a learning community where the interaction between faith and intellect may be explored."[3] Perhaps the clearest evidence of this claim is found in the increasing number of law schools that include in their curriculum offerings a course in law and religion. It must be emphasized, of course, that the curriculum structure, classroom methodology, and faculty profile of a professional school cannot be dictated by a specific religious orientation. When a religious dialogue is distorted into narrowness and intolerance, both education and true religious commitments suffer terribly. An open and free religious dialogue, however, enhances education at all levels and strengthens religious commitments themselves. Church-related colleges and universities prove that every day by providing an education that at its best is genuinely less restrictive than that offered in other institutions.

This author finds it useful to make reference to Mercer University for an example of the relationship between a liberal arts education and

---

[2] Godsey, "The Mission of Mercer University," p. 15.

[3] Ibid.

a legal education because of personal familiarity with the institution. The explanation of the positive impact that church-relatedness can have on a college or university should reassure any reader who is skeptical about whether there is a sufficiently strong relationship between the general educational world and the "world of Mercer" to justify the specific reference to the latter that runs through this analysis. Also by way of explanation, it must be acknowledged that the fact that a liberal and legal education are compatible in their ultimate objectives does not necessarily mean that every liberal arts college will produce a significant number of graduates who are intellectually suited for law school. Nor does it necessarily mean that every law school will take full advantage of the presence of students who already have experienced a high-quality liberal education. Variations in style, teaching quality, and resources make blanket predictions on either point impossible. Yet there can be no doubt that, at their best, a liberal education and a legal education are landmarks along the same path. The liberal component always comes first, however, and thus serves as both a theoretical and pragmatic preparation for law school. As its most basic work, a satisfactory liberal education must develop the mechanical skills that are necessary for success in law school. The loftiest educational aims will remain unfulfilled in the absence of the skills that make them possible. The next portion of this essay will evaluate the skills that every law student must possess on the day that he or she enrolls.

Reading and Writing

Reading is to the mind what exercise is to the body.
(Sir Richard Steele)

You write with ease to show your breeding,
But easy writing's curst hard reading.
(Richard Sheridan)

The successful law student must be able to read and write. That simple statement usually will produce a few chuckles from any prospective law student. A few months later, when the prospective student confronts the reality of legal education, the stark truth of the statement may produce more than a few tears. The law student who cannot read and thoroughly comprehend difficult material that embodies extremely subtle distinctions faces an unfortunate result. The student's troubles will be compounded by the fact that inadequate reading skills invariably will be reflected in an unsatisfactory written product. Evaluations of the effectiveness of particular study habits employed by law students are notoriously susceptible to the twin weaknesses of too much speculation and too little hard proof. Nevertheless, it is obvious that some presumably intelligent law students do not perform well academically despite great effort on their part. If one assumes that not all of these students are the victims of the infamous emotional traumas of law school, then the point raised in one recent analysis of study habits cannot be dismissed.

It might be that style of English usage is the dominant factor reflected in grades, and that a few credit hours of remedial English in the form of advanced expository writing would help many students' grades more than endless hours reading appellate decisions. It seems the legal curriculum ignores students' deficiencies in this area in teaching a profession which deals to an overwhelming extent with language, hoping the preparation of greatly varied undergraduate and high school backgrounds will satisfy the highly demanding standards confronting the attorney.[4]

Surely it is true that an *effective* liberal education will cultivate the high levels of reading and writing skills that are so essential for the study of law. If a liberal education does not do so it will fail not only the students who eventually will pursue a legal education, but many other students who need the same level of skills even though they will never attend any law school. The two initial aims of education mentioned earlier related to the development of clear and precise thought processes and an increased ability to use language in an effective way. Those aims apply to all liberally educated students, not just prospective law students.

The law student who cannot exercise the basic skills of reading and writing in an increasingly sophisticated manner cannot organize, and the law student who cannot organize cannot survive. Like the reading and writing skills on which it rests, the ability to organize large amounts of material is fundamental to success as a law student and in

---

[4]Guy R. Loftman, "Study Habits and Their Effectiveness in Legal Education," *Journal of Legal Education* 27 (1975-1976): 418-22, 448.

the legal profession. Also like the need for reading and writing skills, this point is so obvious that many prospective (and actual) law students tend to forget it.

For a law student or for a lawyer, organizational ability can be defined as the ability to discuss and analyze, either in writing or orally, a wide range of related facts and issues in a manner that will be understandable by an intelligent individual who previously was uninformed, in part or totally, regarding the matter in question. In effect, organizational ability implies communicative ability to such a degree that the two are really synonymous. The "uninformed" individual may be a judge, a juror, another attorney, or (in the case of a student) a law professor. The very first uninformed person that the student or lawyer must educate through his organizational ability is the student or lawyer himself.

Organizational ability should increase rather drastically as a result of the law school experience. It will not increase at all, however, if for many years prior to enrolling in law school a student has been permitted to confuse the self-expression and self-fulfillment that are so much a part of liberal education with undisciplined ramblings. The law student who can read, write, and organize may find himself thinking in a logical way. This rare quality is said to exist even today in a few corners of the world. It is a treasure for any person, but a necessity for law students and lawyers.

Liberal Education and the Study of Law

*Note too that a faithful study of the liberal arts
humanizes character and permits it not to be cruel.*
(Ovid)

In discussing the relationship between liberal education and the study of law, it obviously is not enough simply to acknowledge that the former represents a potential source of students with the intellectual equipment (and perhaps even the maturity) required to deal with law school. Nor is it enough to recognize that the fundamental aims of liberal and legal education are complementary. It is true that a person who is the product of a liberal education should be encouraged by the knowledge that the exotic demands of judicial procedure do not require that earlier days with Keats and Shelley be forgotten forever. The fact remains, however, that the intellectual bonds that join liberal education and legal education cannot obscure the conflicts (both real and imagined) that always seem to have permeated the relationship. In describing the fourteenth century in her well-known book, *A Distant Mirror*, Barbara Tuchman notes that in that long-ago time "lawyers were universally hated and mistrusted."[5] The passage of six hundred years may have reduced the amount of public antipathy displayed toward lawyers, but that antipathy certainly has not been eradicated. Proponents of the liberal arts have never had to endure the sort of gleeful barbs aimed at lawyers by Shakespeare, or the derisive "instant analysis" heaped on the legal profession by the mass media in the wake of the Watergate scandal. On the other hand, liberal educators, at least those in American society, have been compelled to endure continuing questions regarding whether their areas of intellectual endeavor have any legitimacy unless linked to the professions upon which many of their students ultimately embark. It is arguable that the reputation of liberal education in the United States has been affected negatively throughout the country's history by the persistent view that the liberal arts curriculum is not in accord with the American ideology of work—or, more specifically, work for pecuniary gain. That thesis runs throughout an examination of American higher education entitled *The Academic Revolution* that was undertaken in the late 1960s by Christopher Jencks and David Riesman. The explanation given by Jencks and Riesman for the increase in enrollment in the liberal arts since World War II probably is accurate, though it certainly is unlikely to please anyone with a strong belief in the intrinsic value of the liberal arts.

The growth of the liberal arts is partly a matter of more young people going to college, but that is not the whole story. One of the most important changes over the past century, and one that largely offset the rapid spread of professional schooling in the late nineteenth and early twentieth centuries, was the growth in enrollment of women. While some of these coeds simply wanted to earn a teaching license, and others simply wanted to find a husband, they were in general more open to the humane aspects of undergraduate education than men were. Certainly they provided the liberal

[5]Barbara Tuchman, *A Distant Mirror* (New York: Alfred A. Knopf, Inc., 1978), pp. 53-54.

arts professors with larger audiences than they ever had before. Professors have not, it is true, usually welcomed the feminization of their subject. But this says a good deal about the professors' commitment to a higher vocationalism of their own, which judges a student's merit by whether he will go on in the field and discounts women because they will not.

Another important reason for the popularity of the liberal arts is the fact that they have long been, and continue to be, regarded as suitable undergraduate preparation for those callings that delay professional training until graduate school. Thus as graduate professional enrollment rises, undergraduate liberal arts enrollment does likewise.[6]

The "Prelaw Myth"

A lawyer without history or literature is a mechanic, a mere working mason; if he possesses some knowledge of these, he may venture to call himself an architect.

(Sir Walter Scott)

More than ten years have passed since the publication of *The Academic Revolution*, and during that period an unprecedented increase in applications for admission to law schools has occurred (as well as a drastic increase in the number of women who *do not* enroll in the liberal arts simply to earn a teaching license or to find a husband). At the same time, liberal arts colleges have tended to portray their ability to provide good preparation for professional education— especially legal education—as a cornerstone of their attractiveness to potential students. By doing so, they have for all practical purposes adopted the favorable American attitude toward professional studies as a tool for student recruitment. That is a normal reaction to intensifying economic pressures, and by itself probably is harmless (particularly since it happens to be a recruiting technique based on fact). This approach has developed further in two very distasteful ways, however. First, an unpleasant competition for "prelaw" students has developed

---

[6]Christopher Jencks and David Riesman, *The Academic Revolution* (New York: Doubleday & Company, Inc., 1968), p. 200.

among individual academic departments within liberal arts colleges. Any person who spends much time in the law school admissions process is familiar with this phenomenon. Second, liberal arts colleges have developed entirely new programs that seem to owe their existence primarily to the untested (and very dubious) belief that the programs are good preparation for law school. The classic example is found in the various new criminal justice departments that have appeared since the mid-1970s. Criminal justice shows signs, at least at a number of southeastern schools with which this writer is familiar, of replacing political science as the "major of choice" for potential law students. This simply makes an unhealthy situation worse, because the characterization of *any* area of concentration as preeminently suited to preparation for law school is a serious mistake. In its official statement on prelegal education, published in each edition of the *Prelaw Handbook* (a basic source of information on law schools for prospective law students), the Association of American Law Schools[7] (AALS) states its position regarding the quality of undergraduate instruction that is most important for prospective law students:

> That quality of education is concerned with the development in prelaw students of basic skills and insights. It thus involves education for:
>
> • comprehension and expression in work;
> • critical understanding of the human institutions and values with which the law deals;
> • creative power in thinking.[8]

Interestingly, the only reference to specific courses in the AALS statement is made in a negative fashion:

> So-called "law" courses in undergraduate instruction

---

[7]The Association of American Law Schools is literally an association of law schools. It is an accrediting agency, and presently has 136 members. All of the law schools that belong to the AALS also have been approved by the American Bar Association (the other accrediting agency for law schools), but there are thirty-eight (38) ABA-approved schools that have not yet attained membership in the AALS. The AALS functions as the learned society for law teachers, and represents legal education in relations with the federal government and with other educational organizations and learned societies.

[8]Phillip D. Shelton, ed., *1980-82 Prelaw Handbook* (Washington DC: Association of American Law Schools and the Law School Admission Council, 1980), p. 14.

should not be taken for the purpose of learning "the law." They are not intended, and are not likely to be effective, as education for lawyers, although they can be very helpful in undergraduate curricula for teaching students "about law" and quite possibly for helping students estimate whether they might be interested in law study.[9]

As long as liberal arts colleges allow the "prelaw myth" to continue, and sometimes actively encourage its growth, they base their own attractiveness to a large group of students on that myth. Ironically, a genuine liberal education can stand on its own merits as excellent preparation for law school. It does not require support from the "prelaw myth."

The Joint Crisis of Liberal and Legal Education

A liberally educated person meets new ideas with curiosity and fascination. An illiberally educated person meets new ideas with fear.

(Vice Admiral James B. Stockdale
POW, Vietnam
Recipient of the Medal of Honor)

It is impossible to spend much time in law teaching without becoming acutely aware "that some collegians are drawn to the study of law because they yearn for certitude. They want to be told authoritatively what the rules are. They want to be spared unsettling doubt. They think they will be able to take refuge, as it were, in fixed, undebatable law. These yearners for certitude, of course, are going to be disappointed."[10] This problem is as old as the present form of legal education itself, but it has been exacerbated in recent years by an apparent assumption on the part of some legal educators (and justices of the United States Supreme Court) that law schools have failed. Francis Allen, a member of the faculty of the University of Michigan School of Law and former president of the Association of American Law Schools, argues that this inordinately defensive outlook has bred a "new anti-intellectualism" in legal education.

---

[9]Shelton, ed., *Prelaw Handbook*, p. 14.

[10]Walter Gellhorn, "Preaching That Old Time Religion," *Virginia Law Review* 63 (1977): 175-87, 182.

The loss of confidence in intellectually and humanistically motivated law training prepared the way for the rise of a new anti-intellectualism in legal education, new not in kind or quality, but in the breadth and intensity of its expression both in and out of law schools. The new anti-intellectualism insists on what my colleague, Paul Carrington, has described as "instantaneous practicality"; it is impatient with any educational activity that does not promise an immediate and discernable payoff in private law practice. It is concerned primarily with the "how," not the "why." It displays small interest in the substantive issues that confront this society. It reveals a narcissistic fixation on the techniques of the law office and the courts. It views askance the role of the law schools as critics of the law and as sources of new law. It gives short shrift to the obligation of the law school, as an integral part of the university, to discover and communicate new knowledge. It scoffs at "philosophy" as wasting students' time or as incapacitating them for practical affairs. It is not an interest in improved "skills" training in legal education that identifies the new anti-intellectualism; nor is it the desire to equip students for a more humane and effective career at the bar. The essence of the new anti-intellectualism is, rather, the narrowing of interests, the rejection of intellectual and humanistic concerns, the militant assumption that the test of an educational endeavor is its impact on the law firm's ledger. It is characterized by confident but wholly unsubstantiated judgments about the contributions of particular educational experiences to professional proficiency.[11]

Under the impact of what may be rather ephemeral cultural and social trends, and perhaps in their own initial response to the economic tensions likely to result from a declining applicant pool in the 1980s, law schools are beginning to show more than just faint signs of

---

[11]Francis A. Allen, "The New Anti-Intellectualism in American Legal Education," *Mercer Law Review* 28 (1977): 447-62, 450.

succumbing to one of the great misconceptions of modern education. Again to quote Professor Allen:

> One . . . must . . . protest the educational ideology that has pervaded the lives of many university students. The "learning is fun" ideologues have slain their tens of thousands. Learning, in fact, is pain, at least in those aspects of it concerned with the indispensable discipline of basic drill. Paradoxically, learning confers profound satisfactions, and the intellectual life is a kind of play. The pleasures, however, cannot be achieved without experiencing the pains.[12]

Legal educators, in effect, are wrestling with the temptation of following an approach for which (justifiably or not) they have criticized their colleagues in the liberal arts for at least the last decade. This approach equates "the capacity for self-transcendence" that is one of Godsey's aims of education with an abandonment of education itself. Godsey explains that an educated person exercises his capacity for self-transcendence when he "recognizes his limitations and seeks to maintain some measure of distance from his own ideas and beliefs. Otherwise, his own actions and opinions seem to take on a quality of infallibility that is not conducive to the continuation of learning or the development of wisdom."[13] Ideas that survive the crucible of self-transcendence offer guidance to the educated person for his or her entire life. In effect, they become the basic, governing principles by which an individual functions and survives. These principles bridge the gap (wherever one exists) between the world of intellect and the moral world. When an educator concludes that there are no principles by which his work can be directed, when he assumes that the only guiding principle is that there are no guiding principles, he is acknowledging either an intellectual fear or intellectual laziness, or both. In any case, such an educator is incapable of formulating complex substantive ideas and then subjecting them to the crucible of self-transcendence. The educator thus replaces rational self-doubt with intellectual and ethical nihilism. This produces a student for whom the marketplace will be life's only meaningful arena, and actually reduces the range of

---

[12]Allen, "The New Anti-Intellectualism," p. 460.
[13]Godsey, "The Mission of Mercer University," p. 14.

benefits that can be derived from activity in the marketplace. Legal educators, with the zeal of reformed sinners, tend to deplore recent developments in undergraduate, liberal education for exactly this reason. One may hope that, like Professor Allen, more legal educators will have the grace (and the insight) to include law schools in this condemnation. Otherwise, the "myth of legal education" may take its place one day alongside the "prelaw myth."

Index of Names

Percy, Walker, 79
Perry, William, 161
Petrach, 14
Pico, Count Giovanni, 15
Poincare, Jules Henri, 33
Polanyi, Michael, 13
Pope, Alexander, 66

Randall, John Herman Jr., 14
Rather, Dan, 80
Riesman, David, 173, 188, 189
Robespierre, 15
Rodgers, Robert F., 163n
Rogers, Will, 10
Ross, J., 152n
Ross, K. Patricia, 155
Rousseau, J.-J., 15

Saint-Simon, 16
Sanford, Nevitt, 163, 177
Schopenhauer, Arthur, 116, 117n
Schroeder, Charles C., 151n, 152n
Shakespeare, William, 127, 188
Shaughnessy, Mina, 167, 168
Shelley, Percy Bysshe, 187
Shelton, Phillip D., 190
Shils, Edward A., 170
Skinner, B. F., 179
Smith, Mary Lou, 95-101

Socrates, 75
Stevens, Wallace, 137

terHorst, Jerry, 62
Tolkien, J. R. R., 13
Trilling, Lionel, 68
Trinkaus, Charles, 14
Tuchman, Barbara, 188
Twain, Mark, 74

Valla, Lorenzo, 14
Virgil, 127
Voltaire, 15-16
Voegelin, Eric, 17, 20
Volkoff, Vladimir, 21
Vonnegut, Kurt, 136-37
Von Rad, Gerhard, 20
Von Ranke, Otto, 13

Walpole, Robert, 15
Walsh, William Henry, 52
Watts, Isaac, 15
Weber, Max, 174
Wesley, John, 15
Wheelis, Allen, 128
Whitehead, Alfred North, 19
Wilder, Thornton, 13

Yonge, George, 152n

MP Perspectives on Liberal Education

Composition was by Mercer Press Services, Macon, Georgia:
designed by Jane Denslow,
the text was phototypeset on an Addressograph Multigraph
Comp/Set 5404,
and paginated on an A/M Comp/Set 4510.

Design and production specifications:
text typeface—Times Roman (11 on 13);
text paper—60 pound Booktext Natural;
endsheets—Multicolor Antique, Bombay;
cover (on .088 boards)—Holliston Said Cloth (15021).

Printing (offset lithography) and binding were by
BookCrafters, Inc., Chelsea, Michigan.